# A Beautiful Bricolage

# A BEAUTIFUL BRICOLAGE

## Theopoetics as God-Talk for Our Time

SILAS C. KRABBE

Foreword by Loren Wilkinson

WIPF & STOCK · Eugene, Oregon

A BEAUTIFUL BRICOLAGE
Theopoetics as God-Talk for Our Time

Wipf & Stock
An Imprint of Wipf and Stock Publishers
199 W. 8th Ave., Suite 3
Eugene, OR 97401

www.wipfandstock.com

PAPERBACK ISBN: 978-1-4982-9535-2
HARDCOVER ISBN: 978-1-4982-9537-6
EBOOK ISBN: 978-1-4982-9536-9

Manufactured in the U.S.A.                                        07/25/16

For those disillusioned and doubting—
May we still speak

*Would it be a simple coincidence—that poets keep speaking about the same world? Or could it be that they live in the mystery where our Being abides? Poetry: this desperate attempt to say what cannot be said.*

—RUBEM ALVES, *THE POET, THE WARRIOR, THE PROPHET*

# Contents

# Foreword

## by Loren Wilkinson

SILAS KRABBE HAS WRITTEN a book which is both frustrating and important. The frustration comes in part because he is introducing a group of thinkers who are deliberately stretching the conventions of language. The importance is that such stretching is a necessary reminder that all of our words about God are a scaffolding erected around mystery, an attempt to speak about what we cannot speak about. So *A Beautiful Bricolage* has been for me a good chance to think about the language I use about God.

Ludwig Wittgenstein—whose later book, *Philosophical Investigations*, is a major source of Anglo/American philosophy—concluded his earlier book, *Tractatus Logico-Philosophicus*, with a gnomic aphorism that has since become famous: "What we cannot speak about, we must pass over in silence," (in German it is as rhythmic as a poetic couplet: *Wovon mann nicht sprechen kann, daruber muss mann schweigen*).[1] It is the book's seventh numbered proposition, and unlike the first six, which are each expanded with intricate reasoning and symbolic logic, it stands in lonely isolation, like a kind of great secular "Amen."

What immediately annoyed Wittgenstein's positivist colleagues, like Bertrand Russell and the Vienna Circle, was the implication (made very clear in the statements leading up to that concluding proposition) that there were indeed many things which could not be spoken of—*and those were the most important things*: like the existence and nature of God, the meaning of the universe, or the source and nature of good and evil.

All such metaphysical questions, they had hoped, could be discarded as nonsense, leaving for meaningful language only empirically verifiable scientific facts ("The boiling point of water at sea level is 100

---

1. Wittgenstein, *Tractatus Logico-Philosophicus*, 151.

degrees Celsius") or emotive statements (like "ouch!" or "ugh!"). For a while Wittgenstein seemed to take his own advice, retiring from philosophy to work as a gardener in a monastery. But eventually he became, reluctantly, convinced that those various un-sayable things did require speech—which led to his influential teaching at Cambridge, and to *Philosophical Investigations*, published after his death.

That later work—which lucidly explores the many "language games" through which we try to speak of all those things that are central to our being human—provides the framework in which most serious philosophy—at least in North America—is carried on today. Yet there are still in that tradition some who remain annoyed with Wittgenstein for that seventh proposition of the *Tractatus*, and his later violation of it.

And their complaint could well be the grumble of some readers of this book by Silas Krabbe. *If there are indeed so many things that we cannot speak of, why do we still keep trying to speak (and write) about them?* Why not indeed "pass over them in silence"? But what Silas has done here is to provide a kind of guide to a small but important movement of religious thinkers who, while agreeing that the most important things are unsayable—and, perhaps, have been diminished by our attempts to say them clearly—are nevertheless trying to say them in a different way. They are trying to create a tradition of "God-talk" in a time when traditional "God-talk" seems outmoded, irrelevant, or unintelligible. The usual name for that older discourse is "theology." By contrast, the movement Silas describes in the pages which follow has been called *theopoetics*.

There is indeed a respectable Christian movement which carries out philosophy within the somewhat limited space cleared for it in the tradition inspired by the *later* Wittgenstein. It is perhaps best represented by Alvin Plantinga and Nicholas Wolterstorff, who see themselves working in an honorable tradition of Christian clarity that includes Thomas Aquinas, John Calvin, and my longtime colleague at Regent, J. I. Packer. But if these thinkers do engage the "theo-poets" Silas is dealing with, they do so primarily to critique—or dismiss—them.

For they, like the long tradition of Christian philosophy of which they are a part, are committed to clarity: if not the stark clarity of the choice between science or silence (which is all the *early* Wittgenstein allowed), then at least the clarity provided by being clear about the rules of the language games we are playing.

But in this book Silas is introducing his readers to a group of thinkers who—though they sometimes write with admirable clarity and eloquence—do so in defense of the positive value not of clarity but of *mystery*. Stanley Hopper, Amos Wilder, Rubem Alves, Gabriel Vahanian, John Caputo, Peter Rollins, Catherine Keller, Richard Kearney, Callid Keefe-Perry—all of these subjects of Silas's book draw not on the tradition inspired by Wittgenstein (whether "early" or "late"). They are shaped more by the continental European philosophers whose master is Martin Heidegger—and, standing behind him, Friedrich Nietzsche.

Nietzsche is perhaps most popularly known for announcing (through his madman in the marketplace) the death of God. And one of these writers Silas deals with—Gabriel Vahanian—became famous for a book titled *The Death of God*, which gave its name to a widely-hyped movement. (I still recall seeing on a news stand, when I was a graduate student at Johns Hopkins in 1966, the big letters on the black *Time* cover: *Is God Dead?*)

So what impels Silas, writing as a Christian, to title his book on this movement "A Beautiful Bricolage: Theopoetics as God-Talk for Our Time"? And what prompts me, also a Christian—and a former professor of his at Regent College, a graduate school of Christian studies—to call this an important book for Christians to read? My answer to that question has three parts.

First, many Christians—Silas and myself among them—feel that the tradition of orthodox Christian theology, which we both accept and affirm, does not fully express what we sense, feel, and know about God, creation, and ourselves. Especially, in the evangelical tradition, we have tended to value clarity over richness, rather in the tradition of Wittgensteinian philosophy. We believe firmly that God has communicated, both in the biblical record of the long story of the Jews, in Jesus, and in the long history of the Spirit in the church. But we have been too quick to reduce that communication to propositions and logic, forgetting that most of it is in story and poetry, rich with paradox, irony, and metaphor. In Christian history, at least as much has been communicated from and about God in art and music as in words; yet we tend to forget those sources, and thus privilege "theo-logy" over "theo-poiesis." Edwin Muir (a Scottish poet and re-convert to Christianity) described the pattern well in a poem, "The Incarnate One," recalling the rule-bound faith of his childhood. After wondering how we could "betray / The Image" and "the Incarnate One unmake" he laments that "the Word made flesh here is made word again . . ."[2]

To defend *theopoiesis*, as Silas does, in a tradition dominated by *theology*, is to begin to recover the truth that the word (logos) was made flesh. And it only is in and through our flesh and our senses that we experience the fruits of poiesis.

The need for this recovery of the poetic, to balance the logical, is perhaps more obvious now in the second decade of the twenty-first century. Whether or not we are *postmodern*, we are no longer so enchanted with modernity, which developed out of the (false) assumption that we and the world could be understood after the model of the machine. Such a world is perhaps more congenial to theology than to theopoiesis. (Though, as we shall see, in trying to theopoetically correct those dangerous attempts at an unachievable clarity, it may be equally dangerous to leave theology behind.)

A second reason why I have a particular interest in this book by Silas is more personal and autobiographical. The period that Silas is writing about—roughly from the sixties to the present—corresponds to the period of my own efforts (first as a graduate student, then as a teacher and writer) to bring the Christian story (which shaped me from my earliest memories) to bear on the story of Western intellectual culture. Thus I have had to swim in some of the currents of thought he describes and have been shaped by some of their sources.

The "Death of God" movement erupted in the media while I was a graduate student in the Writing Seminars at Johns Hopkins, working on a novel. I was studying there with some of the same professors who, the following year, invited Jacques Derrida to give the lectures at Johns Hopkins which introduced American scholars to "deconstruction," the poorly-named movement which influences several of the writers Silas discusses. So I picked up some of those influences as I read twentieth-century literature.

By nature and temperament I am, I suspect, more comfortable with theopoiesis than theology. So it was with mixed feelings that after Johns Hopkins I began three years of theological study at an evangelical seminary. There I began to learn both the richness (and some of the poverty) of historical theology. I also had as a professor—a brilliant, if somewhat quirky teacher—a Lutheran historian, who combined an interest in the

---

2. Muir, "Incarnate One," in *Collected Poems*, 228.

imagination and the arts with (paradoxically) a kind of Christian empiricism. I first encountered Wittgenstein's *Tractatus Logico-Philosophicus* when he assigned it as the only text for a course in Christian apologetics.

I still profit from the argument he made, drawing from the early Wittgenstein: that knowledge is, necessarily, founded in the senses. Knowledge is not spun out of our heads; it is based in a world we can know, and investigate, and which we share with other knowers. Historical knowledge is no exception: however imperfectly events in the past are communicated to us, they were real events in a real world, accessible to us in the same way any other knowledge is, through investigation (even if second- or thirdhand) of direct experience. He agreed with Wittgenstein: if we have no basis for our theological statements in the world of sense experience, we had better be silent. But, he argued, we *can* speak of God, both theopoetically and theologically, because the story of God's action is also history.

So when (on a bitterly cold night before an overflow crowd in the University of Chicago's neo-gothic Rockefeller Chapel) my professor debated Thomas Altizer, one of the "Death of God" theologians (whom Silas also discusses), it was obvious that my professor had the better logical case, and on those grounds pretty clearly "won" the logical debate. The solid historicity of the Gospels make a strong argument for a God who was—and is—alive. But in many ways the evening still went to Altizer. For he was arguing *theopoetically* as well as theologically. And Altizer was not of course arguing for a literal "death" of God. (It is doubtful that Nietzsche was either.) There was a poetic force in his argument for a radical kenosis, a profound self-emptying of God into human history. The very real logical problems with his argument did not empty it of emotional and imaginative force. Perhaps more important: Altizer came across as a far more sympathetic—and empathetic—person than did my more orthodox professor.

That seminary professor was a supportive supervisor of my master's thesis on the implications of the incarnation for understanding the arts. But he was deeply critical of my own approach to what came to be called theopoetics when I used Owen Barfield to argue that the imagination had epistemological significance—that it helps us both to know, and to shape, what is true. And he later revealed what still seems to me a regrettable insensitivity to the difference between myth and history when he undertook to prove the truth of the Bible by organizing an expedition to Mt. Ararat to find the remains of Noah's ark! Nevertheless, his insistence

that our talk of God is vacuous unless it is rooted in the empirical seems
to me an essential truth. To sever theology *or* theopoiesis from history
still seems to be a fatal move, a conviction I will return to shortly, for it is
relevant to the whole theopoetic project, and hence to Silas's book.

But perhaps my most direct involvement with "theopoetics" stems
from the fact that I did my doctorate—an interdisciplinary humanities
degree, drawing on religion, literature, and philosophy—at Syracuse
University. All of the courses I did in the religion department were with
Stanley Romaine Hopper, recently come to Syracuse, near the end of his
teaching career, from Drew University. Silas calls Hopper the main source
of the movement in theopoetics, in the sixties and seventies, which he
suggests is growing again in importance in our own time.

I met in Hopper a tall, kindly man of great depth and integrity
who (though originally a Methodist minister) showed little interest in
orthodox Christianity. What he was interested in exploring was what he
called "the depth dimension" of human experience. He introduced me
to many writers who continue to be important in my thought—Delmore
Schwartz, Wallace Stevens, Rainer Maria Rilke—and especially, Martin
Heidegger. They enabled Hopper to articulate and illustrate two things:
first, that the world around us is radiant with significance, if we could
only see it; second, that we have it within us to open ourselves to this
all-pervasive radiance, to make our works and our lives (to use a favorite
metaphor from Heidegger) a "clearing in being" around which the mystery of Being will appear.

Stanley Hopper became the supervisor of my dissertation (modestly
titled "Meaning, Man and Earth"). And he introduced to me the important idea which is central to Silas's book: that "theology" is not the only,
or even necessarily the best way to think or talk about God. There is also
*theopoiesis*, approaching God through the imagination. That insight has
informed me profoundly.

At the same time, as a Christian I found Hopper's approach frustrating, for it never got closer to God than the *theo-* in "theo-poiesis."
God was occasionally as specific as "the divine" or "the transcendent,"
but usually seemed to be no more than the "depth dimension" in myself,
or simply the bloom of mystery on the ordinary, the radiance of Being
itself. There was no hint that prayer to such a divinity might ever be an
appropriate response, nor any interest in the history of Jesus, beyond the
*idea* of incarnation (which was suspect because of its Greek-ness). Some

of Hopper's favorite words from Wallace Stevens were these splendid
stanzas from "The Auroras of Autumn":

> There is nothing until in a single man contained,
> Nothing until this named thing nameless is
> And is destroyed. He opens the door of his house
>
> On flames. The scholar of one candle sees
> An Arctic effulgence flaring on the frame
> Of everything he is. And he feels afraid.[3]

That is as close as Hopper (or Stevens) seemed to get to a living God. (I
have often wondered what Hopper would make of the good evidence that
a fully cognizant Stevens, near death, asked for and received the sacra-
ments from a Catholic priest whom he knew.)

A third reason for my interest in Silas's book is that it both illuminates—and is illuminated by—an extraordinarily important recent work
by the Scottish psychiatrist and philosopher Iain McGilchrist. That work,
*The Master and His Emissary*, has been praised variously, by scholars in
both the sciences and the humanities, as "a masterpiece," "a book of the
century," and "one of the best contributions to the world of thought ever
written." Its relevance for Silas's *Theopoetics* is that it provides a good
foundation for a better understanding of the necessity, and the right relationship, of *both* theology and theopoiesis to each other. McGilchrist does
this first by exploring the nature of the way our divided brains engage the
world, then by exploring the cultural world which that engagement has
produced. Thus his work helps us understand the concerns of the writers
Silas is presenting, leading both to appreciation of those concerns—and
caution about their possible misapplication.

McGilchrist's thesis—though it is voluminously researched, supported, and applied—can be simply stated. He argues that we share with
animals and birds a divided brain because we need the kinds of attention that each half gives. On the one hand, the organism needs narrow,
focused attention on things it must use for its survival—a bird needs to
distinguish a seed from its background; a wolf must focus intently on the
deer it wants to kill and eat—this is the kind of attention provided by the
left hemisphere. On the other hand, the organism needs to be open to the
surprising and the new, the unexpected other, in order (for example) to
locate a mate or avoid being prey.

---

3. Stevens, "Auroras of Autumn," in *Collected Poems*, 416–17.

In human beings both these kinds of capabilities are vastly expanded. McGilchrist distances himself from a great deal of popularized fluff
about the hemispheres, both of which are thoroughly involved in almost
everything we do. (There is no such thing as a "right-brained" or a "left-
brained" person.) Nevertheless it is the case that language, reason, and
tool-use are centered in the left hemisphere, and music, empathy, awe,
and metaphor in the right. So we have the capability of paying attention
to the world in two very different ways. The world of the left hemisphere
is a kind of (necessarily) simplified map. In McGilchrist's words:

> This kind of attention isolates, fixes, and makes each thing ex-
> plicit by bringing it under the spotlight of attention. In doing so
> it renders things inert, mechanical, lifeless. But it also enables us
> for the first time to know, and consequently to learn and make
> things. This gives us power.[4]

The right hemisphere world, on the other hand, is a

> live, complex, embodied world of individual, always unique be-
> ings, forever in flux, a net of interdependencies, forming and re-
> forming wholes, a world with which we are deeply connected.[5]

When some of these differences between the hemispheres first began to
be understood, it was assumed that the pragmatic left hemisphere, with
which we "grasp," "comprehend," and make use of the world, was the most
important. It is rather the case, McGilchrist shows conclusively, that most
of what is unique to our humanity—"imagination, creativity, the capacity
for religious awe, music, dance, poetry, art, love of nature, a moral sense,
a sense of humor"—is centered in the right hemisphere.[6] It is (or should
be) "the master." The left hemisphere is meant to be "the emissary," the
servant, of the more empathic right. It simplifies the complexities which
the right hemisphere gives it, reducing them to useful maps and tools for
that bigger, richer vision.

The problem, as McGilchrist shows, is that the simplified version
of the left is more persuasive than the complex visions of the right—but
it leaves out much that is important. It is easy for the person to fix their
simplified clarity as the truth, rather than the open-ended richness of the

---

4. McGilchrist, *The Master and His Emissary*, 31.

5. Ibid.

6. Ibid., 127.

right. Thus (to use McGilchrist's terms again) the servant keeps supplanting the master.

The relevance for the tension between theology and theopoiesis is obvious. We sense God in many ways: first, through the double mystery that there is anything at all, and that we are here to experience it. T. S. Eliot says it well in *The Four Quartets:*

> *The wild thyme unseen, or the winter lightning,*
> *Or the waterfall, or music heard so deeply*
> *That it is not heard at all, but you are the music*
> *While the music lasts. These are only hints and guesses,*
> *Hints followed by guesses, and the rest*
> *Is prayer, observance, discipline, thought and action.*[7]

But we cannot pin down these fleeting senses of miracle and meaning, though we can express them poetically. Scripture itself, which we rightly recognize as a record of revelation from God, is similarly elusive. Jesus acknowledged this when his followers asked for a left-brained explanation of his right-brained parables. He quoted the cryptic words of Isaiah:

> Keep listening, but do not comprehend;
> Keep looking, but do not understand. (Isa 6:9 NRSV)

It is true that Jesus then went on to explain the parable to his disciples. One way of explaining his explanation is to say that he reduced the theopoetic to the theological. Indeed, one might well say that such a reduction explains much of the history of theology, which takes irreducible events and language and builds a frame of concepts around them which makes them easier to grasp. The theopoetic writers Silas is expounding in this book are saying that the conceptual framework has gotten in the way of the mystery it is trying to explain. Such defense of mystery is an important task.

But some cautions are necessary. First, it is important to remember a central point of McGilchrist's analysis: though the simplified maps of mysterious territory which the left brain makes are indeed simplified, and thus can be misleading, they are nevertheless essential if we are to explore the territory. We do need to grasp and comprehend. A very real danger of the theopoetic is expressed in another set of lines from Wallace Stevens that Stanley Hopper (who was, according to Silas, a father of theopoetics) loved to quote:

7. Eliot, "Dry Salvages," in *The Completed Poems and Plays*, 136.

> Throw away the lights, the definitions,
> And say of what you see in the dark
>
> That it is this or that it is that,
> But do not use the rotted names.[8]

That advice is clear enough, and it is clear that he would have included most of Christian theology under what he calls "the rotted names." (See his poem "Sunday Morning.") But it is not good advice. When one is confused, definitions are helpful. When one is in the dark, a light is a gift. The fact that some names are "rotted" does not imply that we can do away with all names.

When one perceives how sometimes what we say about God has become "rotted," it is tempting to say (with Wittgenstein) that we must remain silent about God, or (with Williams) to "throw away the definitions," whether by Paul, or Aquinas, or Calvin.

It is in answering this anti-theological temptation (and thus explaining the true relationship between theology and theopoesis) that McGilchrist's understanding of our bipolarity is so helpful. The part of us which does theology, using the tools of logic and reason to be precise and definitional about God, is a necessary servant to that part which encounters, through the feelings, the darkness and mystery of God. But it should always be the servant of that part of us which encounters mystery through metaphor and imagination. Silas, through his introduction to these theopoetic writers, is calling us to recognize the primacy of the poetic.

My caution to Silas, and to the thinkers he is explaining, is to *not* throw away the "light and the definitions" but to use them as a guide in understanding the inexhaustible mystery which is the triune God. Here I recall the helpful insistence of my quirky seminary professor. If we have no access, through the secondhand but genuine experience of witnesses of the flesh-and-blood revelation of God, we had best remain silent. But we do have such access. As T. S. Eliot continued in those lines from "The Dry Salvages," we *do* have more than "hints and guesses" for

> The hint half guessed, the gift half understood, in Incarnation.[9]

---

8. Stevens, "Man with the Blue Guitar," in *Collected Poems*, 183.
9. Eliot, "Dry Salvages," 136.

At the center of Christian belief is the conviction that "the Word beyond the world," the *logos*, or reason, grasped best perhaps through the abstractions of our intellect, has entered flesh, become part of *mythos*, story. Thus we need not remain silent, for (in the words of John's first epistle) we can speak about "what we have heard, what we have seen with our eyes, what we have looked at and touched with our hands . . . the word of life." That incarnate, crucified, and resurrected one is the source for both theology and theopoetics.

Silas is, of course, well aware of this need for caution. Thus he cites with approval, toward the end of his book, a theopoetic writer, Michael Halewood, who (says Silas) "proposes a cooperative relationship between philosophy and poetry, where the hand touches and the eye sees and the ear hears, and the wound is felt in all of its fullness." Silas is calling us to just such a recovered understanding of the balance of theology and theopoiesis through this "Beautiful Bricolage" of "God-Talk for Our Time."

Silas is trying in this book to defend poetry over logic in order to speak of the unspeakable. An occupational hazard of those of us who make this attempt is to let the mystery which one is trying to defend break the normal rules of writing. Often this is done by breaking words down to the poetry hidden in them—as Martin Heidegger, one of the grandfathers of theopoetics, does (to the endless fascination and frustration of his readers). If, as Heidegger said, "language is the house of Being," and if we are trying to enlarge that house, it might be necessary to do some violence to the vocabulary. Silas does this often—as in, for example, his playing with the way that the root *pli* (which means "bend" or "fold") occurs in such various words as "sim*pli*fy," "com*pli*cate," and "am*pli*fy." Such playful strategies can be confusing.

Thus if the reader is frustrated by the play of language in the opening pages, he or she might profit by turning to chapter 4, "Aims: Not-Answers," where Silas quite lucidly lays out *eight* ("a resurrection number," he points out) goals of theo-poetic writers: (1) Holding Together; (2) Encouraging Exuberance; (3) Giving Space (a translation of the German *Gelassenheit*); (4) (Re)locating Transcendence; (5) Embodiment; (6) Protecting the Individual; (7) Defending Human Agency; (8) Favoring New Life.

Silas, in his defense of *theopoetics*, is calling us to all of these good things. You will find this a challenging and rewarding book.

## BIBLIOGRAPHY

Eliot, T. S. "The Dry Salvages." In *The Complete Poems and Plays*. New York: Harcourt, Brace and World, 1952.

McGilchrist, Iain. *The Master and His Emissary: The Divided Brain and the Making of the Western World*. New Haven: Yale University Press, 2009.

Muir, Edwin. "The Incarnate One." In *Collected Poems*. London: Faber & Faber, 1979.

Stevens, Wallace. *The Collected Poems of Wallace Stevens*. New York: Knopf, 1969.

Wittgenstein, Ludwig. *Tractatus Logico-Philosophicus*. Translated by D. F. Pears and B. F. McGuiness. London: Routledge & Paul, 1966.

# Acknowledgments

FIRST, I WOULD LIKE to thank a former professor who believed in my abilities early on during my undergraduate studies. Not only did she affirm my curiosity and intertwined streams of thought, Gay Lynn Voth was the first person to tell me that she was excited to one day read my first book. I am not sure if she will remember saying that, but nevertheless those few words left an indelible mark that guided my study through many a dark night. In addition to imparting the value of precise academic rigor amidst a plethora of options, she encouraged exploratory study that traveled widely and tangentially—even if those forays toward peripheral ideas made others uncomfortable. The principal thing, however, that she both taught and lived was to bring one's whole being—emotions, physicality, passions, fears, and above all a love for people and the world—into one's work so that the work becomes shaped by love and is given as a gift to those affected by it. It is my hope that in the following pages there are insights, connections, and an intellectual generosity that will make her proud, but mostly I hope that she sees small reflections of herself scattered throughout what follows—evidence of her tutelage continuing to impart wisdom many years later.

My church community also deserves some well-earned recognition. In many ways this book is shaped by and is for my church, even though many of those I see weekly will never read a word of it. The reason for this disconnect is not due to a lack of interest, rather it is the result of significant barriers of social and economic marginalization due to racism, mental illness, cycles of poverty, trauma, and addiction. Consequently, reading a complicated text on theopoetics is in stiff competition for time and attention against survival in an urban subsistence-living context. Nevertheless, it is with those individuals and within that faith community that I have been given the freedom to think through many ideas, experiment with method, and utilize much of the material presented in this book. It is with them that I find myself situated, and they have always been a curious, engaged, and in their own way critical audience; and I am a better person and thinker because of them. Additionally, they are the best living reminder that I am loved in both my successes and brokenness, and for that I am ever grateful.

I am indebted to my friends, family, and companion for sticking with me through my highs and lows and continually sharpening my mind with questions, debate, and late-night conversations. They remind me to retain some semblance of balance in my life, thereby helping me practice what I preach, and in so doing they protect me from myself. I hope that they enjoy reading this book, and I look forward to their piercing critiques offered in a way that only those who know me and my inconsistencies well will be able to do.

I would also like to acknowledge and thank my editorial team for their critical eyes, close reading, probing questions, requests for clarification, and attention to detail, without which the final version of this book would include many more of my oversights. The friendship, keen minds, wit, ruthless argumentation, and endless hours of editorial efforts by Duncan Ris, Ryan Kelley, and Janina Mobach are a testament to iron sharpening iron.

Finally, I would like to express my gratitude to Loren Wilkinson, not only for authoring the foreword to this book, but also for affording me significant leeway as a student. Without his encouragement to pursue my own interests, whether through flexibility facilitating seminars or orchestrating guided studies, I may never have wandered down the various intellectual pathways necessary for compiling the survey recorded within this book. Furthermore, I am ever grateful for his grace and the spacious place made available to me by always allowing me to view the word count for a paper as a minimum or a mere consideration. Without such leniency and generosity this current project would never have grown beyond its germination in my mind. Mostly, however, I thank him and his wife, Mary Ruth, for their friendship, guidance, honesty, and holistic approach to life and education. I have gleaned much more from them, their table, and their open door than I can adequately express here.

# Pre-amble-ing

*It is not theology.*
*Theology wants to be science, a discourse without interstices . . .*
*It wants to have its birds in cages . . .*
Theopoetics *instead,*
*empty cages,*
*words which are uttered out of and before the void,*
*the deep sea (the eyes look upwards, waiting for the light which fractures*
*through unquiet waters . . .),*
*deep forest (if one has patience one will hear the voice of an enchanted*
*bird who lives there—and yet it has never been seen by anyone . . .),*
*empty cathedral, where our thoughts become light and jump over abysses*
*. . .*
*Exegetes and hermeneuts are at a loss.*[1]

—RUBEM ALVES

THEOPOETICS IS A NEBULOUS nebula. Both the term and the material to which the term refers are expansive and vacuous, substantive and event-ive, beautiful and bewildering.[2] Like a nebula, how one perceives theopoetics will depend on how one refracts, polarizes, and assigns meaning to the material. For there is much more going on within theopoetics than an aesthetic exterior. In the same way that images of nebulae appear differently to the human eye when analyzed and assigned a perceptible color at discrete points along the electromagnetic spectrum, theopoetics also

1. Alves, *The Poet, the Warrior, the Prophet*, 99.
2. Theopoetics and nebulae also share in drawing our minds to origins: "Theopoetics began when our capacity for language emerged, and it has been fleshing itself out since." Harrity et al., "Theopoetics of Literature," 6–7.

1

appears differently depending on what lies in focus. It is my intent to make visible a wide range of theopoetic light, but not so wide as to lose sight of the amplitude, crests, and troughs of the wavelengths. I hope my chosen polarization will enable an appreciation of some of the depth that is always present within the theopoetic discourse—a depth perhaps not immediately visible upon first glance—without forfeiting the scope of the material.

Before the late twentieth-century and early twenty-first-century manifestation of theopoetics, which is the focus of this book, one might posit that there is a theopoetic tradition that dates back to early Christian expressions, or to Judaism, or even the first articulations of a religious awareness itself—that is, if by theopoetics one broadly meant either the connection between poetic writing and theology or poetic writing about God / the divine. While such an inquiry would be far beyond the scope of this book, permit me to indulge my imagination in a very brief journey through my account of "Theopoetics: A (Very) Brief History."

Probing the cosmic microwave background radiation of origins is always a risky expedition. For often such a mission, back to beginnings, may only lead to more unfathomable depths. There is no guarantee that the trip one undertakes into these complexities will include a return, thereby becoming an odyssey; instead one may always be partaking in perpetual departure. Likewise, one can never be assured that delving into history will offer anything more than initial impressions like a speedy stolen single glance at a taboo picture. Yet gazing through a nebula, beyond a two-dimensional image appetizing to the eye, one may find that a certain *je ne sais quoi* arises and becomes absent. The eye may tentatively taste what perhaps lies beyond, but it will never be fully satiated. This present absence may implore something deep within the viewer, marshalling a call for both more to be said and more to be depicted—so too this foray into origins. For within the Christian tradition, from which I write, there is an origin, or at least an origin story with which to begin. Genesis has a certain *je ne sais quoi*. It begins with rhythms, with vibrations, with assonances and onomatopoetic resonances of the *tehom* and *tohuvabohu*, with the watery womb and the wild waste, which are rhythms awaiting their reason (which is not so different from quantum indeterminacy and superstring vibrations—trajectories toward which this origin may, or may not, lead).[3] Yet it is only a moment after one hears this hum that the vibrations explode into speech and the reader is thrown forward.

Stumbling ahead, trying to catch a footing in this wet and wild that is becoming a firm *terra nova*, the reader may realize that the story of theopoetics might touch down everywhere, or nowhere. I, therefore, can only mention a sample of the possible theopoetic resonances within the Bible and the Christian tradition. For after exploring origins, the poetics of the biblical narrative history dances onward with its scenic, subtle, and succinct communication.[4] Furthermore, the obvious poetry of the Psalter and Wisdom literature and the rhetorical flourishes of the Prophetic books may set one's feet to dancing. The narrative structures of the Gospels (e.g., the seven signs and the seven "I Am" statements in John), the hymnlike qualities of the Epistles (e.g., Phil 2), and the angelic songs of Revelation (e.g., Rev 15) also integrally unite tempo, form, and function as aspects of their speech.

These poetic articulations of rhythm and verse do not cease with the closing of the canon. Augustine's *Confessions*, its framing structure of a prayer (i.e., confession as both praise and prayer), may also be considered poetic.[5] Even the great castle structure of Thomas Aquinas's *Summa Theologiae* has a poetic/aesthetic characteristic in its expansive structure. Furthermore, one might also experience a moment of poetic, transcendent bliss when coming up for a breath in the middle of Karl Barth's *Church Dogmatics*. In such a moment one may perceive in a new way the macro-argument in the micro-configuration because Barth's trinitarian and christological structuring pervades all aspects of his work, which

---

3. Keller argues that *tohuvabohu* is best translated "waste and wild" for "its onomatopoetic rhythm and rhyme." This translation then assists in cross-disciplinary conversation since "matter, as we are learning from a new physics, *is* at base rhythm. Indeed, superstring theory 'suggests that the microscopic landscape is suffused with tiny strings whose vibrational patterns orchestrate the evolution of the cosmos.' The earth *tohuvabohu* suggests a rhyme that has not yet found its reason." Keller, *On the Mystery*, 49. Furthermore, Keller deepens the necessity for life as a form of reason in such a context when she writes, "Apart from the spirit 'brooding o'er the chaos,' Tehom remains a sterile possibility and 'God' remains mere Word, fleshless abstraction and power code. Only through pneumatology does theology have a prayer." Keller, *Face of the Deep*, 233.

4. Provan et al., *Biblical History of Israel*, 91–92. John Walton also makes a similar case for the poetic aspects of narrative history to be acknowledged in his comparative study of ancient Near Eastern thought. Walton, *Ancient Near Eastern Thought*, 227–37.

5. Marion, *In the Self's Place*, 13–32.

means his structure and content communicate in a synergistic manner.[6] And if I were to stop with just those three, I would neglect dancing behind Gregory of Nyssa as he follows Moses into the darkness of the cloud, and miss falling in line with Dante Alighieri's footsteps that pursue Virgil and Beatrice, and lose sight of Tolkien's subtle description of hobbit feet. Alas, there are too many instances to count! For in all of these examples one can see and hear, when considering the tradition widely, that the poetic and aesthetic aspects of theological reflection are not a frivolous note of a fringe minority, but rather a prominent and repeated chord.

However, for the remainder of this book *theopoetics* will be defined and engaged much more narrowly in scope. That is, theopoetics specifically refers to the way of doing theology and reflecting upon the divine that began to develop in the second half of the twentieth century and is currently experiencing something of a revival in the early twenty-first century. Yet even within the examined timeframe, the works here considered are not exhaustive of the topic, although I do consider them to be a fair representation of the diversity of those utilizing the term theopoetics.

Having said this, I note two particular weaknesses regarding what follows. First, the authors and works engaged with below predominantly write from positions of academic power within a North American context. Second, and relatedly, a disproportionate number of male authors are considered. Both of these weaknesses are in part due to the accessibility of materials, the makeup of the field itself, personal limitation with respect to language proficiency, and my own ignorance. By stating these weaknesses openly it is my desire to provoke further writing and study that will give greater attention to voices left unheard in this current work.

The thesis of this book is rather simple: theopoetics is a relevant and viable option for contemplating, discussing, and speaking the divine in the early twenty-first century. However, rather than arguing for this thesis explicitly, my goal is to persuade you, the reader, of this thesis through a survey of the discourse. I will attempt to situate theopoetics in its context of the late twentieth and early twenty-first centuries, appreciate the questions being asked, map out and expose some of the many folds within the conversation, highlight some of the desires, and analyze some of the perimeters.

To borrow a metaphor from Catherine Keller—who in turn develops Nicholas of Cusa's use of it, who borrows it from Gregory of Nyssa,

---

6. Barth, *Church Dogmatics*. For example, §9 "The Triunity of God" is constituted by three parts: "Unity in Trinity," "Trinity in Unity," and "Triunity."

who comes to it by meditating on the life of Moses—I will attempt to evaporate the reader into a cloud of theopoetics. It is a cloud because no two authors define the term in precisely the same way, which means that there is proximity of particles (i.e., definitions) but no identification. The cloud is visible, but as one draws near, it becomes apparent that neither the edges nor the substance are firm or defined and that to grasp or contain the cloud is not achievable.

However, within this cloud it is possible to loosely identify two strata: those of theopoiesis and theopoetics; between which there is difference, but no complete separation.[7] David Miller highlighted this difference in an article "Theopoetry or Theopoetics?" in which he asserted a firm distinction. Miller's argument in brief is that "the problem [i.e., the death of God] requires not a turn to uses of poetry and other arts to bring to expression a traditional theology [theopoetry]; rather, the 'crisis' of the death of God requires a radicalized poetics in the face of nothingness, i.e., the no-thing-ness of ultimate reality [theopoetics]."[8] While Miller's distinction is apt in identifying two trends within theopoetics, "theopoetry" as a term failed to gain traction, and authors have continued to use the term "theopoetics" where Miller would classify their thought as "theopoetry."

I, in turn, favor Keller's distinction between "theopoiesis" and "theopoetics," both of which are actually used by authors of theopoetics.[9] "Theopoiesis" is Keller's term for what Miller calls theopoetry but with an extra focus on poiesis as making, in addition to utilizing poetry, aesthetic language, and other arts as the approaches through which to convey reflections regarding the divine. In order to understand this *making* more fully it will be helpful to quote Keller at length as she meditates on *becoming* in relation to beauty as development/making:

> The aesthetic significance of the very word *becoming* has often been missed: In English the verb has an odd transitive form, related to the adjective *comely*. We say, "That shirt *becomes*

7. Keller, *Cloud of the Impossible*, 309.

8. Miller, "Theopoetry or Theopoetics?," 11.

9. Keller considers Miller's division a "cunning distinction" and makes use of it herself because it helps show that "theopoetics, in other words, has everything to do with the art and form of poetry. But it is not reducible to a literary style." Keller, "Theopoiesis and the Pluriverse," 185. Yet even Keller does not retain "theopoetry" as a term and moves on to "theopoiesis" and "theopoetic" in later work; see Keller, *Cloud of the Impossible*.

you"—as though beauty results from something becoming part of another, from some participatory genesis. (The shirt is so right for you, that shirt is you!) In other words, if theopoiesis means the human becoming divine through the divine becoming human: God *becomes* us. That God is comely, becoming, in us—clothes us in beauty. It is in *becoming* that we become divine.[10]

While Keller's theopoiesis entails a more active element than does Miller's theopoetry, both agree that theopoetics refers to a type of response to the death of God.[11] However, the division between theopoiesis and theopoetics remains flawed insofar as many of the individuals who Keller might categorize under theopoiesis use theopoetics to refer to their own work. As such the dividing wall between these two strata remains more permeable than firmly set.[12] Keller goes on to explain how she understands the relationship between the two categories. In her opinion, when the two strata encounter the "wall" within the cloud, it is experienced not as something meant to divide so much as to be leaned into, a response that allows for imperceptible nearness without identification.[13] This understanding shall become slightly clearer in the discussion regarding her thought below.[14]

I offer an apology to the reader that within this differentiation offered by Keller the meta-level (theopoetics) and one of the terms of the micro-level (theopoiesis and theopoetics) share the same word, which may cause some confusion. However, rather than create a new designation, I have decided to retain what appears to be the usages within the field itself, even though this may cause the cloud of theopoetics to darken at points rather than shine with luminous clarity.

---

10. Keller, "Theopoiesis and the Pluriverse," 192–93.

11. Keller rearticulates Miller's understanding of "theopoetics" this way: "Theopoetics begins not where theology *ends* but where it *negates* itself. This is actually where it *comes to be*: where it negates itself *becomingly*." This distinction is helpful in reframing the "death of God" as one form of God, or one idea of God, which theopoetics comes after, but not as a complete annihilation of "God." For further clarification see the "Death of God" section of this book in chapter 3. Ibid., 187.

12. See my appendix, in which I attempt to categorize the authors referenced in what follows into these two groups, remembering that the division is somewhat permeable.

13. Keller, *Cloud of the Impossible*, 101.

14. Also see the section on Catherine Keller in chapter 3.

Clouds, permeable walls, and evaporated terms; theopoetics is not for those who want to see clear divisions, but it might be for those who want to hear resonances between particles. In theopoetics the border between terms is cloudlike and therefore will be most appreciated by the reader who drifts with the cloud and listens for the faint echo of a harp at those blurry moments rather than attempting to focus too narrowly or categorize too firmly.[15] The cloud of theopoetics and the distinctions within it require you, the reader, to adopt something of a "learned igno-rance" in an apophatic moment that does not intentionally mystify terms but rather accepts that the dividing wall between terms becomes a chias-mic fold.[16] In doing so, you will yield to the ineffability of a folded cloud, in which there is imperceptible nearness—without identification—and also a chasm of what seems like an infinite depth between the two sides of the fold. Furthermore, in plumbing the depths of such a fold you are likely to find other folds within the fold: it is a com*pli*cated cloud.

*A note to the reader*: I hope that it is already apparent that I am playing with a few theopoetic ideas, methods, and themes within this book. I have used them ahead of their clarification in subsequent sec-tions in hopes that you, the reader, will have a variety of *Aha*! moments throughout this book, where you say to yourself, "Oh, now I see what Silas was doing!" For example, the notion of writing as play shall become clearer when we explore the work of John Caputo and Jacques Derrida. Other theopoetic ideas I play with are the fold (*plia/ply*—in words like sim*pli*city, multi*pli*city, etc.), extended metaphors, mixed metaphors, asides addressed to the reader, structured writing (both meta and micro), embodiment (physicality and aspects of time and space), de-construction of W/word(s), slipping between languages, holding the reader in an idea, and returning to words, concepts, and phrases. All the while, however, I

---

15. Various writers make use of theopoetic flare and slipperiness of language to greater and lesser extents, so identifying those engaging in theopoetics is very subjec-tive and largely due to self identification by the author.

16. Keller, *Cloud of the Impossible*, 22. Rather than "learned ignorance" that Keller uses Alves instead writes of "unlearning," which *mutatis mutandis* is the analogue to a cultivated disposition of "mindful unknowing"—not to be confused with a willful ignorance. Given this analogue I do not think that it is merely coincidence that Alves plies the fold in a similar way to Keller: "To explicate: from the Latin 'explicate', a verb derived from 'plicare' which means 'to fold'. To explicate: to eliminate all folds where darkness abides; to spread the text out, so that the light will illuminate the whole sur-face. . . . I became sure that I was no longer a good teacher when, instead of turning the lights on I preferred to turn them off." Alves, *The Poet, the Warrior, the Prophet*, 8.

hope to retain clarity of argument, not obfuscating more than the subject matter requires. It is my hope that you enjoy reading this work and exploring the topic as much as I did writing it.

Furthermore, in this book as I attempt to map out some of the contours of theopoetics I will necessarily be engaging with themes of mystery, imagination, sensuality, the non-"rational" and alternatively conceived "rationality," and with freedom, flux, and flow, which coincide with the decline in the hegemony of "method."[17] As such, it would seem disingenuous to flatten out all of these wonderfully diverse landscapes into the static two-dimensional contours of a gas station paper map. Therefore, I resist stating a regimented method of inquiry, and instead, I intend to exercise some of the freedom and play that theopoetics liberates both the author and reader to utilize while rejecting the confines of positivism, propositionalism, and the supremacy of method.

What I do produce is a web of entanglement, in which I draw connections—both tangential and sequential—and perceive echoes, resonances, and allusions. Not all threads are followed to their end because that is not the point. My point rather is to be caught up into the middle of theopoetics and to see where some of the threads are anchored in theology, phenomenology, metaphysics, linguistics, culture, and philosophy. To take the metaphor further, you, the reader, are a fly that finds itself blown into the midst of the web; what follows is the fly surveying the surroundings, assessing how it came to be entangled and beginning to take stock of the situation/discourse it finds itself in. Yet in the end, I do not think this is a pernicious web with a black widow waiting in its center, but rather it is a gracious web that bounces, stretches, upholds, and provides seemingly endless possibility to be explored, such that one life is not sufficient to thoroughly test and understand all of the strands.

*I have pulled on Ariadne's thread, from where I always already am. I've done my best to follow the line, but the line seems confused. Maybe I followed a "decoy" or fray? Perhaps. But it seems to me, from where I stand, that it was not a thread but a web. What appears to be a fray was not, but a joint. Maybe it is a cyclical web, and if I just choose a different direction I'll find my way out! . . . Alas, it seems that this web is not two-dimensional but three-dimensional, and I am entangled beyond escape. Always, Already, Beginning, Anew, Again.*

17. Hans-Georg Gadamer, for one, saw the restrictions of applying a strict method as potentially being prohibitive for encountering truth. For more on theopoetic method and hermeneutics, see the subsection on Caputo in chapter 3.

While I do not want to lose the complexity and entanglement of the web, I have chosen to order the deep web of theopoetics as a fold in this book. So, where am I taking you? We are on a chiasmic adventure into the fold. Why, you might be wondering, has there been so much throat clearing in this pre-amble prior to the introduction? Because the introduction itself begins a descent into the theopoetic fold—it is a slippery surface, and I wanted to offer you, the reader, something of a thread, a life preserver, a pre-flight safety announcement, and a map, before entering the chaosmic deep, the cloud, and the entangled web in which the game of theopoetics is played.[18] Therefore, I present to you a menu of the fold before us that tells you what is about to come (insofar as I am able to offer such an assessment of the *to come* or claim mastery of my own writing— for more may be unfolded or refolded than even I intend).

> Beginning
>> When and where is our moment?
>>> What do we want/wonder?
>>>> Surveying the setting: What led us here? What does it look like?
>>> Where do we hope to go?
>> Where can we not go?
> Ending

This chiasm guides the following adventure into theopoetics. It is not a "choose your own adventure," nor is it a detailed instruction manual. For assistance in making your way between those two I offer this folded map, which may be pulled out and referred to if you begin to feel dizzy or disoriented staring down a fold with no foreseeable crease at the bottom

---

18. I have been quite taken by the word "chaosmos" ever since I came across it my first time reading a book by Caputo. Since then I have found myself utilizing it, referring to it, and resting in it as I attempt to make sense of my own existence, depressions, joys, and hopeless moments surveying the world. I find in this word a harmony that rings true to my experience of life and its shrouded tune is often more soothing than a brilliant light. Caputo's usage of the term helps explicate its usefulness as well as its meaning: "We all start out in a situation of indecipherable complexity and we are not so sure where we are heading, much less how to get there. Catherine Keller, one of the leading American theologians of the day, helpfully compares deconstruction on this point to chaos theory, which describes how a certain optimal state of chaos must be an ingredient in a system if the system is to be productive. Not simple chaos, not flat out anarchy, which produces nothing, but what James Joyce (again!) called a 'chaosmos,' a chaos-in-cosmos, an ordered disorder, where the tension between the two is set in a delicate balance that allows the system to generate new and unforeseen effects." Caputo, *What Would Jesus Deconstruct?*, 52.

to aid you in a subsequent assent, or drifting away in a cloud with nothing to grasp, or drowning in water too turbulent to swim in, or entangled in a web of words to the extent that you no longer know where you are coming from, or playing a game for which the rules are ever changing.

# An Introduction: Why Theopoetics?

*This way of thinking had visible effects in their way of walking. Just by watching how a person walked it was possible to identify the group to which it belonged. The villagers went around hopping and dancing, as children do, which was an expression of how they felt inside: light creatures, with winged bodies. The Enlightened, on the contrary, were solemn and grave and marched with steady steps, slowly, testing the ground to see if it was a firm foundation. This difference was also visible in the ways they spoke. The villagers made use of poetry and by the use of metaphors they jumped over immense abysses of time and space; from apples to childhood memories, from a wheatfield to a golden hair, from fish-cleaning to deep rivers of love, from bread and wine to the body and blood of a beloved person, absent. The members of the sect, on the contrary, moved from one word to another only after they has succeeded in building solid bridges of evidence and proof. "We must proceed carefully," they never tired of saying. It was then that someone realized the close relationship which there exists between ways of walking and ways of speaking. Poetry is dancing; prose is marching. It is obvious that the members of the order were very much afraid of the embarrassment of stumbling, a risk which one has to run if one wants to dance.*[1]

—RUBEM ALVES

JEAN-LUC MARION ARGUES, IN concert with Augustine's *Confessions*, that when one truly speaks about God, one is speaking *to* God not merely speaking *of* God. For as one speaks a word, one speaks after the giving of the word, and therefore if one is truly speaking of God, one is addressing God as locutor, and in so doing one becomes the interlocutor since one

---

1. Alves, *The Poet, the Warrior, the Prophet*, 67.

always speaks after God.[2] So too in theopoetics, as one speaks *to* God and *of* God, one speaks before and after all at once. Language, a gift of words, from the Word, is put into play, which binds together the locutor and interlocutor as a world of meaning is formed in between the two. Such a space of formation is an in-between, shaped by the W/word(s) and worlds before and provoking the words and worlds after. As I enter the discourse of theopoetics, I likewise speak before and after those who have already written on the topic. Most notably in this work I attempt to write before and after L. Callid Keefe-Perry.

Keefe-Perry has written an excellent primer on theopoetics, mapping out various stages, developments, and styles as well as introducing key writers in the discourse. Keefe-Perry uses a method of "showing" or allowing the authors to speak for themselves.[3] This method aligns with the "heart" of his book, which is "the belief that how we articulate our experiences of the Divine can alter our experiences of the Divine."[4] By letting the authors "speak for themselves" the reader is able to hear the "how" and not merely the "what." I hope to, in my own way, allow for such a hearing.

In an effort not to duplicate Keefe-Perry's excellent work with my own commentary, while still showing that theopoetics is a relevant and viable option for God-talk in our time, I will be focusing on three tasks: one that comes "before" Keefe-Perry's work, one that overlaps, and one that comes "after." Regarding the former, it is my intent to situate the theopoetic conversation in a slightly larger framework of the history of Western Christian thought and highlight the questions theopoetics seeks to answer. This contextual work will allow me to accomplish my overlapping tasks, which are to identify, survey, and focus on some divisions, explore folds, and to chart some ostensibly irreconcilable elements of the theopoetics, which will entail locating various authors in the waters. With our charts of the theopoetic waters in hand we will navigate the final task, which is an exploration of the aims and confines of theopoetics as explicated by those involved. As such, I will only be working sequentially through authors in the middle section, laying out their thought, categorizing, and assessing it. While in the rest of the book I will use,

---

2. Marion, *In the Self's Place*, 18.

3. Keefe-Perry, *Way to Water*, 8.

4. Ibid., 6.

reference, utilize, compare, and return to the authors and their particularities as I see fit.

In contrast to Keefe-Perry's approach that moves chronologically (time and personality) through individual authors, my macro-structure works primarily spatially (folds) through thematic aspects of theopoetics. While I do spend significant time considering the thought of individual authors in the middle section, this is secondary to my larger approach. Keefe-Perry's assessment, therefore, will probably be regarded as "clearer," more straightforward, analytical, and tailored to the Western mindset; as such it is indeed an easier route into the material. At times—largely influenced by Alves, Caputo, and Keller—I take on a more rhapsodic style; a bricolage of free play as a way of offering more priority to the *how* than the *what* of theopoetics. Again, I am not intending to obscure clarity merely for the purpose of doing so. But I am increasingly convinced that the structure, the rhetoric, and the moments of precision and clarity must serve their purpose within a larger framework that resists conventional constraints of propositional, geometric, and analytic forms of argumentation.

Let me explain. Rather than macro-sections of articulation, analysis, and application (three "A"s), I will flip-flop, flow, and fold (three-point-five "F"s) the material (articulation, analysis/assessment, and application) together. In letting the "A"s become the "F"s and the "F"s become the "A"s, I hope to participate with Alves in unlearning and dis-ordering.[5] It is my hope that this dis-ordering is something of a cruciform upheaval, and a kin-dom re-ordering, wherein the valleys are raised up and the mountains brought low.[6] It is an upheaval that reaches toward a different/difference or *différance* (differing (between) and deferring (delaying)), as a way of being-in-the-world that continually overturns whatever might be.[7]

How does theopoetics accomplish all of that: *différance*, cruciform upheaval, and re-ordering? If I may posit a tentative position: such agency is possible because theopoetics attempts to speak at the intersection of

5. Alves, *The Poet, the Warrior, the Prophet*, 3–19.

6. See Tripp Fuller's chapter "Abba Says, 'Drop the G'" for a fun and informative argument for removing the hierarchy and patriarchy associated with *kingdom* in favor of *kin-dom*. Fuller, *Homebrewed Christianity Guide to Jesus*, 41–63.

7. Derrida, *Of Grammatology*, 23. See also Heidegger, *Being and Time*, 53: "The compound expression 'being-in-the-world' indicates, in the very way we have coined it, that it stands for a *unified* phenomenon. This primary datum must be seen as a whole." Page numbers refer to the German pagination.

spiritual and material reality without compromising either side and without simply defaulting to anagogical interpretation that focuses spiritual readings on heaven or eternal life, readings which often are too quickly conceived of through an antiquated metaphysically-structured mental framework. By eschewing such mental constructs some theopoetics hold the reader in the lurch, flux, and flow of life long enough to provoke real change. While notoriously difficult to define, theopoetics might helpfully be understood as an embodied way of thinking, speaking, writing, and experiencing, which form—as Martin Heidegger might call it—a way of being-in-the-world. Therefore, as noted in pre-amble-ing, theopoetics is more than a hybrid of theology and poetry. Rather, and here I defer to Keffe-Perry's excellent quotation of J. Denny Weaver: "It is an entire way of thinking. From the side of poetry, it shows that ideas are more than abstractions. They have form—verbal, visual, sensual—and are thus experienced at least as much as they are thought."[8] Cultivating this way of being-in-the-world is what then enables the theopoet and the reader of theopoetics to shape new realities.

Caputo offers, perhaps, the simplest definition of theopoetics by way of contrast. He states that "theo-poetics" is "a complex of narratives, parables, and paradoxes of which Jesus is the center piece," in contrast to "a 'theo-logic,' [that is] an ethics, or a church dogmatics."[9] Such a definition, however, requires subsequent redefinitions when it comes to terms such as *truth*:

> A poetics is not true the way the propositional form "S is P" is true, if and only if there is an SP out there that this sentence picks out as if SP were something that a reporter with a video camera who was on the spot at the supposed time and place would have recorded. A poetics is not true the way a scientific theory is true, as a covering law that is weakened, altered, or refuted by the accumulated weight of evidence and replaced by a competing scientific theory. A poetics is true with the truth of the event; it wants to *become true*, to *make itself true*, to *make itself come true*, to be transformed into truth, so that its truth is a species of truth as *facere veritatem*.[10]

8. Keefe-Perry, *Way to Water*, 2.

9. Caputo, *What Would Jesus Deconstruct?*, 57. Caputo later enhances his definition of theopoetics: "By a poetics I mean a collection of metaphors, metonyms, narratives, allegories, songs, poems, and parables, indeed and assessment of *all* the rhetorical strategies we can summon, in order to address the event." Caputo, *The Folly of God*, 94.

10. *Facere veritatem* = showing truth, or doing truth, or making truth happen.

Thus truth is redefined from abstraction into becoming—from death to life.

This creative, generative, and life-giving aspect of theopoetics is reflected in the word itself. Keefe-Perry states "theopoetics" is created by "combining the Greek *theo* with *poiein*, meaning 'to make or shape.'" "Theopoetics," he continues, "is a means of making God, of shaping experience of the divine, and the study of ways in which people come to know the Spirit."[11] In this way theopoetics moves beyond Matt Guynn's initially helpful and broad definition—"a style of writing or theological stance, an artful way of working with language and worldview"—because theopoetics functions; it does not merely state or explain; it is not merely word games.[12] Guynn, himself, expresses and deepens the theopoetic move beyond sim*ply* articulating a thought, or describing an experience, toward what was im*pli*cit in the above definition when he writes, "*theopoetics,* opens up a space for unanticipated dreaming in which the past, present, and future are re-shaped as we reorganize and even re-create our own stories and our relationships with others, the world, and the Divine."[13]

---

Caputo, *The Weakness of God*, 118. An event, for Caputo, does not *exist* (in an onto-theo-logical state); events *insist*: see Caputo, *The Insistence of God*, 82. Therefore, to describe an event is an elusive task, for events are "what we cannot see coming," and they "are not what happens but what is going on *in* what happens" (82–83). Thus, the event spoken of by Caputo is different from Barth's event of revelation as a transcendental occurrence within space-time that corresponds to an eternal decision in the will of God: see Barth, *Church Dogmatics*, 2:262. Caputo's event is also different from event in process theology, in which events are occasions that make up stable entities: see Cobb, *Whitehead Word Book*, 23. (For more on process events see chapter 1 and the subsection on Catherine Keller in chapter 3). Caputo's event is "something *je ne sais quoi*, something going on *in* what I desire" (Caputo, *The Insistence of God*, 84). Events are always contained *in*, but not *by* their signifiers. They are unique in that their effect is larger than their cause. It is in relation to this event that a poetics makes sense for Caputo: "A poetics is the discourse proper to the event, because the event is not a form or structure to be delineated, not an essence or a prestigious presence, not one of the powers that be. An event is not a being in time or outside time but a being spooked-by time. . . . Theopoetics concerns something that has no proper name, since names are nominatives, while a poetics gives words to something coming, something infinitival" (*The Folly of God*, 106).

11. Keefe-Perry, "Theopoetics: Process and Perspective," 579–80.

12. Guynn, "Theopoetics: That the Dead May Become Gardeners Again," 99.

13. Ibid. In *The Folly of God*, Caputo articulates in his own way a proximate movement toward function and action when he writes, "As theology becomes theopoetics, theopoetics becomes theopraxis. Theology wanes into theopoetics and theopoetics waxes into theopraxis. The waning of the logos is the waxing of the praxis. That means that the weakness of God requires our strength to make God whole, and the folly of

While theopoetics in many ways mirrors a romantic response to enlightenment categories, it is not only that; and while theopoetics includes aspects of poetry, it is not just adding aesthetics to classic theology. For theopoetics is not just poetry but performance—it requires performative action in order to come to be: words require a writer writing and speech requires a speaker speaking. Amos Wilder highlights why the active aspect of theopoetics is important: "We speak about a theopoetic because the theme of divinity requires a dynamic and dramatic speech. Divinity has to do with the glory of God and the creature's participation in it. But this means participation in his life and activity and this is something other than passive mystical illumination or epiphanies of the sacred."[14] Therefore, it is precisely the dynamic life of God that activates an active aspect of theopoetics. An example of the activeness of the *how* of theopoetics, in addition to the *what*, is evident in Sam Laurent's thesis of his essay "Kierkegaardian Theopoiesis: Selfhood, Anxiety, and the Multiplicity of Human Spirits" as it is precisely this active aspect that he highlights. He writes, "Kierkegaard's sense of poiesis extends beyond the rhetoric of selfhood to the very process of being an authentic self in his thought."[15] Thus, Laurent argues that for Kierkegaard, selfhood is reconfigured from a solid state to "an active process of becoming."[16] Theopoetics, then, is more than merely something one does external to oneself, but it is a transformative discourse one *participates in* and reciprocally experiences as *being participated in.*[17]

One's full participation in the activity of theopoetics is important because it has to do with the formation of identity: we are formed by our texts. Judith Lieu, when considering identity and textuality, astutely observes that it is in the nexus between oneself and the text that identity is formed. She writes,

> Texts construct a world; they do this out of the multiple worlds, including textual ones, that they and their authors and readers already inhabit and experience as "reality"; that new world itself becomes part of subsequent "reality" within and out of which

God is to let so much depend upon us" (119).

14. Wilder, *Theopoetic*, 12.

15. Laurent, "Kierkegaardian Theopoiesis," 47.

16. Ibid.

17. "A theopoetic poem concerns both inward spiritual depth and outward physical existence, and sacrifices the importance and prominence of neither." Harrity et al., "Theopoetics of Literature," 8.

> new constructions may be made. Yet this is not a self-generating system: constructions and worlds interact and clash with others, whether they are seen as congenial or as alien.[18]

As such, it is not only the life of God, but the life and formation of each human that moves toward an active, dynamic textuality.

In many ways Lieu's understanding of how texts interact echoes Hans-Georg Gadamer's merging of horizons. For Gadamer the interaction between the horizon of the text and the horizon of the self is not merely psychic transposition of meaning or understanding from one to another.[19] Rather, there is a creative moment as the two horizons meet. But the relationship is not merely the meeting of two because both the text and the self are themselves constructed and *pli*able; therefore, the relationship and interaction between them is far from set or determined. This *pli*ability of the self is not a new idea; for example, Karl Marx already highlights the human's constructible identity in his "Theses on Feuerbach." In Marx's articulation, it is clear that anthropology is not entirely deterministic, but it is what might be called dialectically determinable or fluidly constructible. In the third thesis Marx states, "The materialist doctrine that men are products of circumstances and upbringing, and that, therefore, changed men are products of other circumstances and changed upbringing, forgets that it is men who change circumstances."[20] Here Marx argues for a type of dialectic: humans are determined, but humans also have agency and can change their circumstances. In connection with the production of texts, the *what* and the *how* are important for the one who writes theology. For both the mode and the content provided by the author/theologian make up the textual circumstance and will end up shaping and constructing the reader whose horizon merges with the given horizon of the text.

Theopoetic writers actively acknowledge the merging of horizons and the identity formation that occurs in the creative space between them as an invitation for writing to provoke more writing.[21] This invitation is not to mere repetition, but rather it is to participate in writing as a

18. Lieu, *Christian Identity in the Jewish and Graeco-Roman World*, 61.

19. Gadamer, *Truth and Method*, 413.

20. *Marx-Engels Reader*, 144.

21. As Keefe-Perry quotes Scott Holland, "Good theology is a kind of transgression, a kind of excess, a kind of gift. It is not a smooth systematics, a dogmatics, or a metaphysics; as a theopoetics it is a kind of writing. It is a kind of writing that invites more writing." Keefe-Perry, *Way to Water*, 67.

forging of new ideas within this profound sense of human embodiedness. Recognizing humans are more than mathematically rational creatures, theopoetics is concerned with the linking of words and bodies as a means to persuade, to move, and to change a fluid world. Therefore theopoetics affirms an analogous dictum from Marx in his critique of Feuerbach: "The philosophers have only *interpreted* the world, in various ways; the point is to *change* it."[22] Similarly, the theopoet might exclaim: "the theologians have *explained* God, but the point is to *experience, transform, and move* with God." However, to effectively move with God requires knowing the context in which one is moving.

22. Marx and Engels, *Marx-Engels Reader*, 145.

# Chapter 1

# Where Are We? When Are We? —Situating Selves

*I woke up as the sun was reddening; and that was the one distinct time in my life, the strangest moment of all, when I didn't know who I was—I was far away from home, haunted and tired with travel, in a cheap hotel room I'd never seen, hearing the hiss of steam outside, and the creak of the old wood of the hotel, and footsteps upstairs, and all the sad sounds, and I looked at the cracked high ceiling and really didn't know who I was for about fifteen strange seconds. I wasn't scared; I was just somebody else, some stranger, and my whole life was a haunted life, the life of a ghost.*[1]

—JACK KEROUAC

GHOSTS—MINE AND YOURS—SLEEP IN long-ago vacated hotel rooms, dorm rooms, bedrooms, and cribs. In each of those (death)beds remains a ghost when I rise to live. And at night I reunite with that ghostly vapor of a prior self and it sooths me back to sleep. But what of those times I do not re-turn in the midst of my day, and my movement leads me on to an else-where, where I find a different bed? What of the vapors to which I never return? Are they lost? Do they search for me, or I for them? How many may I leave before none is left, and I am but a hollow shell? For you and I are always on the move: crawling, walking, running, riding,

---

1. Kerouac, *On the Road*, 17.

19

trotting, galloping, rolling, driving, flying, and rocketing out into space. With every new move a little less vapor is left, and I fear that leaving is happening at ever increasing speeds. For when I would crawl, I was slow though able to re-turn to my ghost, but now nothing is fast enough. The wheels of the cart, train, and car never revolve quite fast enough; even the propeller and the jet do not quench my thirst for speed. Left behind are the wisps of a ghost I no longer know, and I am never going back.

Mine and yours—we press on and telecommute, spreading ourselves wire thin. But wires were too cumbersome and slow, so we dis-connected and sent messages through the air, through the lingering vapors of our previous selves, to satellites in the sky. Messaging alone was not enough, we needed more: more mobility, more speed, more distances covered and locations *slept* in. So we made pocket computers that accomplish all of our tasks while resting in multiple locations all at once. Now we hurtle down the information highway even when we are defecating. We are slow and fast, present and absent, everywhere and nowhere—all at once.

Where then is stability? Where are our foundations? Where are our unchanging concepts? Where now are our platonic forms amidst this motion? Nowhere, that is where! As we tear ahead at incredible rates, we are fractured by the speed of life; our souls seep out of the crumbling forms and drip like tears all along the way. Our glory, our weighty *kavod*, is spread out like heavy oil drops on a highway. Snapchats, Instagrams, Tweets, and status updates stream live up into the information cloud where they create our ideal timelines. We create our own *ideal forms* with Photoshop and store them in the bits and bytes of the cloud. We are oily tears spread along the highways of life becoming evaporating droplets; we are everywhere and nowhere—all at once!

Spread so thin, we are barely able to think. But if we did, we might wonder, *Will the cloud turn into a thunderhead? Is there a way through this thin spot? Is there a way to let our ghosts re-gather and catch up? Is there a place to be, where our ghostly souls will not be spread so thin, a place in which we can dwell?* To which one might hear the response, *Perhaps. Perhaps there is a way to let our ghosts catch up and our souls condense, a way for the cloud to offer a warm spring rain rather than a destructive storm, a more human, walking-way of being-in-the-world. But only if—perhaps.*

*Perhaps* is a favorite word of Caputo, and in a compact little book— written for the average reader, *Truth: Philosophy in Transit*, he offers a compelling case that humanity's increasing mobility not only affects our existential angst of having our souls left behind, but that this movement "has in fact precipitated a crisis in our understanding of truth."[2] From Immanuel Kant, who never left his hometown of Königsberg, to Derrida, who traveled constantly around the world and would intentionally get himself lost in a new city upon arrival, Caputo constructs a survey of Western intellectual history that draws a correlated development from static location and absolute Truth to movement and situated truths.[3] Rejecting a nostalgic return narrative, Caputo seeks a way forward into the faster paced realm of *truths*, a realm where philosophy and religion are not as distant as they used to be, where many truths are spoken and where theopoetics might play.[4] If Caputo is correct that our physical movement throws into turmoil our conceptions of what *true* means, or what *rational* means, then perhaps *play* is the best way to move ahead as the Western world enters a time of reconsidering where we are, when we are, and what all of our rapid movement means.

Those participating in theopoetics are very involved in exploring what the world looks like from a viewpoint that takes seriously situatedness. Such an approach moves beyond the hegemony of *The Rational* or *The Truth* (for which capitalization is always implied as though referring to an absolute or a proper name of an entity), which are common in the Western world and often live on in uncritical parlance due to often unexamined assumptions. Yet while exploring this world these thinkers by no means assume such exploration to be easy or simple. Wilder reflects on our complicated predicament: "The Enlightenment means liberation, but this liberation is part of the metaphysics of subjectivity and objectivity. We have replaced the teleological schema of antiquity, which confined individuals to assigned places within the system, with a new complex of evils, of subjective individualism, on the one hand and a spreading objectivism on the other."[5] Thus, for Wilder, the Enlightenment results in an increased freedom and movement, but this has apparently paradoxical ramifications of both flagrant subjectivism and outrageous objectivism coexisting. Paradoxical binaries such as these appear to be a common outcome of Enlightenment thought. Theopoetics by being post-Truth and pro-truths makes a task of trying to tackle these schismatic binaries

---

2. Caputo, *Truth*, 1.

3. Ibid., 2, 72.

4. Ibid., 257–62.

5. Caputo, *Radical Hermeneutics*, 256.

by moving beyond what would be the antithetical construction of pro-Truth and anti-Truth.

Gabriel Vahanian communicates this common goal of theopoetics well: "What is needed is to get rid of dualism, particularly if theology is to be liberated both from the analogy of being and its twin, the dialectic of the sacred and the profane."[6] Vahanian's assertion about the necessity of deconstructing binaries, however, does not come from nowhere, nor does it negate clear thought by becoming infinite relativism. Theopoetics avoids meaninglessness by insisting that in order for thought and communication to be *actual* thought and communication they must still be clear, lucid, and *rational*, not impenetrable and utterly opaque. However, theopoetics at the same time does not hold to the binary assumptions prevalent in much of the Western intellectual tradition: yes or no, good or evil, being or nothing, presence or absence, true or false. Instead, rather than communicating through the abstractions of *logical* sequencing that depend on premises of a substance metaphysic that many have disavowed, theopoetics responds, generally, by communicating ideas in a different mode that is more aligned with an embodied human.

The disavowal of substance metaphysics, which is actively part of some theopoetics, draws upon Friedrich Nietzsche's profound dismantling of metaphysics. In "On Truth and Lies in a Nonmoral Sense" (1873) Nietzsche incisively argues a substance separation in Kant's Copernican revolution of the mind—that the viewer and the viewed are intimately connected—to its logical end point: "All we can actually know about these laws of nature is what we ourselves bring to them—time and space, and therefore relationships of succession and number."[7] Nietzsche then follows this development up in *Human, All Too Human: A Book for Free Spirits* (1878) stating, "It is true, there might be a metaphysical world; one can hardly dispute the absolute possibility of it," but as earth-bound creatures, we have no way of knowing about it without revelation.[8] Therefore, a theopoet can say alongside Nietzsche, "*Logic*, too, rests on assumptions that do not correspond to anything in the real world."[9] This assertion regarding logic means that when one is reconsidering God, revelation, and the underlying metaphysics (or lack thereof), one is also considering

---

6. Vahanian, *Theopoetics of the Word*, 46.

7. *Nietzsche Reader*, 120.

8. Ibid., 163.

9. Ibid., 164.

and playing with the logic and associated *rationality* that are connected to one's understanding of revelation, metaphysics, and proper discourse. It follows then that if one removed metaphysics, or changed a metaphysic, one would alter what is *logical, rational,* or able to be called *Truth.* Therefore, as theopoetics entertains radical thought and the deconstruction of previously held assumptions, all of the subsequent aspects are placed into a state of play.

For example, the logical maxim of non-contradiction—that two things cannot occupy the same space at the same time—reflects a substance metaphysic.[10] But this presupposition is placed into question by recent science, which challenges the assumed position that Einstein's theory of special relativity and quantum mechanics "cannot both be right" because the first requires precision that the latter does not allow for.[11] However, Keller, as one example, offers a way forward by rejecting a substance metaphysic and uses an alternative event-based metaphysic instead.[12] In so doing she successfully reframes the apparent contradiction between special relativity and quantum mechanics. By focusing on events coming to be through numerous actualizations of occasions—rather than presupposing permanent, underlying substances as the base materiality of existence—she demonstrates that neither "substance" exists until the moment the possible becomes actual, which means the actualized version of the contradiction never takes place in time.[13] This alternate understanding of existence then has an emancipatory effect for theopoetic

10. "Science, after all, inherited from theology the metaphysics of separate substance, supernatural and natural." Keller, *Cloud of the Impossible,* 131.

11. Ibid., 132–33.

12. An event metaphysic, such as Keller's, begins with the assertion that reality at its base is a *coming to be,* not set matter or substance. Reality then, in an event way of thinking, is a sequence of occasions that come to be in time, which leads event metaphysics to focus on dynamism, movement, and change. I contrast this way of thinking informed by a process of *becoming* to that of substance metaphysics, which are more concerned with static and stable entities that are said to *exist* or *not exist.* NB: this usage of *event* is different than Caputo's use of event, which is an articulation of a phenomenological experience. Reduced for a simple articulation of the difference between these two usages: metaphysics begins with a proposal about the basis of reality and then articulates an explanation of reality in light of this proposal while phenomenology begins with human experience and the perception of these experiences by human consciousness. As such phenomenology is primarily descriptive in its task. For more on Caputo's usage of *event* see the introduction and the subsection on John Caputo in chapter 3.

13. Keller, *Cloud of the Impossible,* 143.

writing because multiple potential meanings, which may have classically been understood as contradictions or paradoxes, can find resolution in the act of reading that actualizes the potential meanings.

An instance of how an altered relationship between possibility and actuality plays out in theopoetics is in Richard Kearney's early twenty-first-century work, *The God Who May Be*. In this text Kearney argues for an onto-eschatological, rather than an ontological or eschatological hermeneutic, thereby placing assumed logical premises in question.[14] Specifically, he writes, "Whereas the ontological play refers to the 'power' of the Same returning to itself, eschatological play refers to the powerlessness of the other, summoning us beyond the Same."[15] Thus his eschatological hermeneutic removes the premise that the Same will return to the Same (Same = Same); instead, he makes room for the beyond (Same = potential difference). This overturns long-held premises of Greek thought in favor of a postmodern disposition toward difference. The postmodern preference for difference is often linked to critiques of Same = Same in that such homogeneity often leads to ethnocentrism, oppression, or exploitation of others who are different. For Kearney, therefore, the eschatological (temporal) hermeneutic is not *irrational* but simply aligned with a different rationality that functions on a different logic, which he argues is more akin to poetics and "the possible God" or "the God-who-may-be."[16] After he is able to free himself from an ontological hermeneutic by way of an eschatological hermeneutic, he then returns in a different way to an onto-eschatological hermeneutic that would not have been possible had the premises of the ontological hermeneutic not been loosened by post-metaphysical (or alter-metaphysical) thought.

While Kearney's onto-eschatological hermeneutic is quite cerebral, Keller offers a more visceral way forward by deconstructing binaries through theopoetic metaphors of the body. For example, regarding light and dark in Genesis she writes,

> Why does God call the light good, and not the dark? Doesn't that prove that [Karl] Barth is right on this—darkness biblically is evil?
>
>     I don't see how. *Elohim* exclaims with delight at the light—it is the new thing, the unfolding of a new order, the explication by word of this universe. How does that make the *implicate*

14. A further discussion of Kearney's work appears below in chapter 3.

15. Kearney, *The God Who May Be*, 106.

16. Ibid., 5, 7.

order, the mysterious potentiality, from which it comes *bad*? Is the womb evil because the infant snatched lovingly from it is "good"?[17]

The logic Keller is arguing against only works if one is operating out of a dualistic framework. Emanation, or a substance metaphysic, necessitates that if one thing is good, the other must be evil (or some privation thereof) because two substances cannot occupy the same *good* space. Against this, Keller's embodied analogy undermines those assumptions and thereby declares two seemingly opposite things good.

Caputo goes beyond deconstructing binaries by redefining rationality as the ability to be understood.[18] He arrives at this conclusion by arguing that "if there is no truth in the sense demanded by metaphysics, if metaphysical truth is dead, then the signifier has been emancipated, set free into its essential element beyond grammar and logic and onto-theo-logic."[19] If there is no ultimate metaphysic, then "there is no privileged native land or native language of thought."[20] It then follows that Western metaphysics, developed from the Greek tradition, no longer holds pride of place. Such an assertion may be terrifying, or deeply freeing. For Caputo, the lack of an absolute metaphysical truth means "the saving message is that there is no saving message."[21] Radical freedom opens alternatives to onto-theologic discourses, and by demoting one metaphysic, it raises the level of all other discourses and systems of thought. The speedy death of metaphysics tears down metaphysical idols that have delineated the parameters of acceptable discourse, and this death has had the resurrectional ramification of opening wide the doors to the *truth* arena. This iconoclastic stance toward metaphysics now requires from humanity that we consult many diverse opinions, all of which ought to have equal freedom of expression so long as they can be understood. As such, Caputo rapidly moves into a post-foundationalist framework of thought where reordering and bricolage is the name of the game.

---

17. Keller, *On the Mystery*, 56.

18. Caputo notes how Gadamer's work was influential in freeing *reason*: "In Gadamer, reason is emancipated from the rule of method and becomes a more plastic, flexible, and spontaneous faculty of application, or perhaps better, appropriation of norms which are at best only general schemata for new and idiosyncratic situations which cannot be anticipated in advance." Caputo, *Radical Hermeneutics*, 210.

19. Ibid., 186.

20. Ibid., 184.

21. Ibid., 186.

One might object that in this fast-paced game of bricolage there needs to be some rules of the road or some criteria for assessing outliers. *There must be a meta-set of rules that state how to deal with data acquired! Mustn't there?* I will let Caputo respond at length from a segment on how the natural sciences are dealing with this question:

> Now one might think that there are certain meta-paradigmatic criteria in terms of which paradigms can be judged and directly compared with each other—like accuracy, consistency, scope, simplicity, and fruitfulness. But although everybody is willing to accept these "criteria," [Thomas] Kuhn argues, they are utterly ineffective in resolving conflicts. Indeed, they conflict with one another, so that we can get accuracy only by sacrificing fruitfulness, or conversely. One paradigm is better in one regard but not another. In the end, scientists have to choose which criteria are more important to them and where they want to concentrate their labors. These criteria, it turns out, are not hard and fast rules but very high-altitude scientific "values" which are of no practical use. Everybody can agree about them without agreeing about what to do.[22]

These *values* thereby return us to Caputo's redefinition of *rationality* in that these discourses do not dismiss the ability to be understood, rather they reject a finalized framework for determining how to arrange the pieces of data or absolute guidelines for weighing the data—bricolage is already the reality. Caputo's postmodernism, therefore, is not antirational or wildly relativistic, but rather it is the full game put in motion: "I would say at this point reason is put *in play* with the matter at hand, that it moves along the way (*Weg*), is put effectively in motion (*Be-wegung*)."[23]

Such a movable game is partially what transports Caputo, and other theopoets, toward the poetic and increases the weight with which it is incorporated into the game. Once movement has loosened the rules, the poet can make a daring entrance. Drawing on Heidegger's poetic thinking, Caputo describes the poet's daring this way, "The poet is obviously a subversive, an outlaw, an enemy of the state and the king, one of those apocalyptic voices which are bent on stirring everyone up. The law says that nothing is without reason, but the outlaw poet says that the rose is without why."[24] The poet is willing to risk the rules, to place reason with-

22. Ibid., 218.
23. Ibid., 219.
24. Ibid., 224.

in the game, and this is not a fruitless move, argues Caputo, for poetic thinking "achieves a relationship with the world which is more simple and primordial than reason."[25] Poetry is more malleable to movement and the movement of bodies; therefore with poetry "we take a leap off the stability of the ground, the solidity of presence—terra firma—and we land in the flux!"[26] And landing in the flux is a good thing because "when the chips are down, reason finds itself without the help of established rules, on its own, in free play, in motion, in *kinesis*."[27] The poet is already running, is on the train, and is cruising the information highway, while Reason appears to have been caught in a solid state with its trousers down.

While loosening the grip of binary thought and redefining rationality are probably the most significant cultural trends with which theopoetics is engaged and to which it is responding, there are other aspects of culture that theopoetics often encounters. Wilder, in *Theopoetic*, a series of compiled articles published in the early 1970s, offers keen insights for understanding and situating the historical moment of theopoetics' arrival and why he thinks theopoetics is the way forward in this context. Of primary importance for Wilder is the imagination as an integral aspect of Christianity. He argues that his time (the seventies) is a wasteland for the imagination, which then renders Christianity unable to respond to the rapid motion of the age because a response requires imagination and a freedom to "generate its own contemporary communication."[28] Therefore, theopoetics, insofar as it can cultivate a new religious imagination, offers hope to what he sees as a bleak dreamscape that informs reality, which has come about due to a vapid social imagination.

Wilder, by questioning how the Global West has arrived at this point, draws a connection between popular Western culture's lack of imagination, expressed in its inability to form new language, with a theological deficit. He writes, "In our own climate both rational criticism and biblicist literalism have reflected a common penury of imagination. It is not surprising that the secularist today neglects the Scripture or is led to some similarly wooden view of its bearing on modern issues."[29]

25. Ibid.
26. Ibid.
27. Ibid., 226.
28. Wilder, *Theopoetic*, 3.
29. Ibid., 49–51.

Wilder then does not mince words when stating his case for the origins of his contemporaries' lack of imagination. It is a section worth quoting at length:

> I repeat that it is a mistake to hold the Puritan tradition or Calvinism particularly responsible. The pragmatic temper of our whole society has more to do with it. If one looks for religious antecedent one should look not to our earlier Calvinist roots but to the consequences of the great revivals of the nineteenth century. Though this widespread movement encouraged emotional expression it channelled such emotion in intense but narrow syndromes which eclipsed all wider sensibilities."[30]

In sum, Wilder's argument is that it was not a total repression of religious imagination and sensuous experience that was detrimental, i.e. Calvinism, but a hyper-narrowing of such expressions into a defined spiritual locale. This pragmatic narrowing to retain a cloistered locale consequently relinquished the rest of the social sphere to further pragmatism (primarily economic and utilitarian). Once pragmatism dominated the social sphere, it turned and also dominated the already narrowed religious sphere, which could no longer resist the larger, more influential social imagination. In this, Wilder identifies the pervasive attitude of his cultural moment that is resistant to imagination, or what some might consider as the nonrational due to a narrow definition of rationality.

Wilder goes on to identify the coupling aspect of his culture, which is an intense focus on the pre-rational. When the religious imagination had retreated from the large social sphere, what might be called the private sphere became fascinated with the unconscious.[31] Wilder writes that there are "many evidences in our culture of a turn toward what we can speak of loosely as the mystical, the prerational, and the imaginative."[32] The psychoanalysis of Sigmund Freud and Jacques Lacan were in vogue (and continue to be in vogue in certain segments of culture and Christianity—for example Peter Rollins's "pyrotheology," his recent book *The*

---

30. Ibid., 50.

31. The awareness of and fascination with the unconscious is present throughout theopoetics. Hopper, in a 1967 essay, "Symbolic Reality and the Poet's Task," already identifies the unconscious as an important dimension: "There is, however, another dimension here, which the poets have long understood, but which the philosophers have been slow to acknowledge. It is the dimension of the unconscious as it relates to the ego-consciousness in symbolic formation." Hopper, *The Way of Transfiguration*, 106.

32. Wilder, *Theopoetic*, 6.

*Divine Magician*, or Tad Delay's *God Is Unconscious* all interact with various psychoanalytic developments often in a poetic manner).[33] Such inquiries into the unconscious arose from, and only further deepened, the schism between the public sphere's lack of religious imagination and a detached private consciousness. Moreover, Wilder links the suppression of the imagination by pragmatism to the bubbling up of a religious desire in alternative locations, which included the growth in popularity of eastern spirituality and *spirituality* in general.

Often linked to the spirituality of the counterculture, the late twentieth century was a time defined by looking to get high. Capturing the many dimensions of getting high, Wilder, writing during the seventies, states, "At no point is this [desire for faith in contrast to skeptical culture] clearer than as regards the inarticulate hunger for plenitude, for transcendence, even for ecstasy both within and without the religious institutions . . . they are at present either in Pentecostalism or in the counter-culture."[34] He later calls this pervasive feeling "the current thirst for spiritual liberation in our society."[35] This "thirst" was, and continues to be, pervasive as people seek ecstatic moments in a number of ways. Wilder, addressing this search, states, "Today, we are confronted with ambiguous cults of ecstasy and Eros in both unsophisticated and sophisticated quarters."[36] While the seventies were a time of euphoria, the shadow side and death of the culture of plenitude are portrayed in films like Dennis Hopper's film *Easy Rider*. Now in the twenty-first century, it is apparent that the drug and euphoric counterculture never truly went away, as humans continue to seek speed, height, and general excess. Recently one can see this yearning reincarnating itself in attempts to transcend physicality via technological media, transhumanism, interstellar travel, and virtual realities.

Theopoetics arises out of this context of getting high. Therefore if theopoetics is also just an attempt to get high, or escape the confines of rational discourse, thereby implicitly fostering a degrading view of the body or materiality and promoting escapism, then I would be forced to conclude that it is of no value. However, within theopoetics there is a strand of radical, (near) materialist theopoetics—that of Caputo, Rollins,

---

33. Keefe-Perry, *Way to Water*, 93–99.
34. Wilder, *Theopoetic*, 9.
35. Ibid., 59.
36. Ibid., 60.

or in many ways Alves—which is focused on the material world and uses theopoetics to approach, rather than flee from, material existence. Nevertheless, it remains a valid concern that theopoetics may amount to nothing more than grasping for loftiness. For if this yearning for preeminence were indeed interwoven within theopoetics, then those involved in theopoetics might find themselves caught like the disciples gazing into the sky, only to hear, "Why do you stand looking into the sky?" (Acts 1:11).[37]

It is not merely my personal disdain for escapist thinking that rails against a retreat to otherworldliness, for the dangers of grasping for height are not limited to a cognitive escapism into the ethereal, but they manifest and actualize within the material world in more substantive forms.[38] Insofar as theopoetics is involved in the critique of metaphysics, it participates in countering the amplitude of this second type—that of humanity's tendency to establish hierarchies. One can grasp for height in a number of ways, sometimes by seeking to soar into the sky on the wings of words or, strangely similarly, by falling into the sublime within theopoetics.[39] Equally problematic would be reading a limiting hierarchical metaphysic into a text and then establishing this singular reading as authoritative and constructing reality in relation to it. Replacing transcendence with hierarchy can be done unthinkingly and at its worst, when applied, it might look like this:

---

37. Mounce and Mounce, *Zondervan Greek and English Interlinear New Testament*.

38. While I agree with Jürgen Moltmann and Jon Sobrino that an ultimate eschatology (*telos* perhaps), sometimes misunderstood as a height or escape, is necessary to judge and contradict the present order of things in order to demonstrate that the present order of reality is not ultimate, here I focus more on a second danger that arises once one acknowledges an ultimate other than the present order of things: it is the danger of attempting to establish what one perceives to be the ultimate. For Sobrino this is the danger of conflating the kingdom of God with the church and thereby losing the ultimate hope of the kingdom, which as an eschatological hope necessarily "stands in contradiction" to the present: see Sobrino, *Jesus the Liberator*, 110–34.

39. For more on the interesting corollary that is the sublime see the section in chapter 5 on the middle.

| Psalm 121* | A Song 12:01pm |
|---|---|
| Assurance of God's Protection | A Lament |
| A Song of Ascents. | A Song of Dissent. |
| [1] I lift up my eyes to the hills— | I lift my eyes to the skyscraper— |
|     from where will my help come? |     oh you who never help me! |
| [2] My help comes from the Lord, | My master and I thy perpetual slave, |
|     who made heaven and earth. |     who made you high above and me below? |
| [3] He will not let your foot be moved; | You won't ever let me lift my own foot; |
|     he who keeps you will not slumber. |     your surveillance state keeps tabs on me. |
| [4] He who keeps Israel | Your economic structures |
|     will neither slumber nor sleep. |     never cease to oppress. |
| [5] The Lord is your keeper; | The welfare state is my keeper, |
|     the Lord is your shade at your right hand. |     it keeps me hidden from view. |
| [6] The sun shall not strike you by day, | It limits access to the elevators of power, |
|     nor the moon by night. |     keeping the subways clear for transportation. |
| [7] The Lord will keep you from all evil; | The powerful know what law is best; |
|     he will keep your life. |     they will determine my life. |
| [8] The Lord will keep | The powerful will establish order |
|     your going out and your coming in |     and will tell me where to go and what to be; |
|     from this time on and forevermore. |     the status quo prevails, forever and ever. |

\* NRSV.

Such a reconstruction of a psalm clearly demonstrates the potential violence often done to a text by the reader—often unconsciously—when interpreting transcendence primarily as a metaphysic of height and power-over another and then translating that height to structural and social hierarchies through theological, political, economic, social, and cultural decisions about *right order*. Insofar as interpretations like the one I ex*pli*cate above are problematic because they create—consciously and unconsciously—oppressive systems, it is encouraging that theopoetics is at least attempting to grapple with such realities of height, metaphysics, and transcendence.

Within this cultural context there is a movement, or degrading, of transcendence from a beyond to a . . . ? It is left as a question mark because there is no consensus regarding how to conceive of transcendence or infinity. Some of the many options are a strong reassertion of transcendence classically conceived of as an *above* or *beyond* (platonic tradition), as a spiritual overlapping realm behind a veil (N. T. Wright), as a depth dimension within the immanent (Martin Heidegger, Paul Tillich), as an infinity between aspects of immanence (Immanuel Levinas), as a transcendental above (Kant, Barth), as temporal infinity (Wolfhart Pannenberg, Alfred North Whitehead), as an unfoldable fold (Gilles Deleuze), as a rupturing event within language (Derrida), as the mystery of words (Vahanian), or as the wonder of the sensuous and the void (Alves). To say the least it is a perplexing relocation.

While one might initially react to some of these options as *reductions* of transcendence, Mike Grimshaw, in the introduction to Vahanian's *Theopoetics of the Word*, helps pinpoint the dilemma that the modern world faces in this regard and why a reconsideration of transcendence may not be as reductionist as it would seem at first glance. Grimshaw, rearticulating Vahanian's argument from *The Death of God*, states, "One can become religious, or more so, participate in religiosity, one cannot, in Vahanian's shocking indictment, become a Christian."[40] He goes on, "This is because we now live in an immanent culture, not the transcendental worldview of Christianity."[41] Christian expressions of faith, therefore, are "unnatural because they exist in neither the traditional transcendental plane nor the contemporary immanent plane; rather they exist in what would be termed the plane of nostalgic religiosity, attempting to make an absent or [functionally] dead God relevant."[42] However bleak this may sound, Vahanian argues that Christianity is adaptable and translatable to various cultures, therefore it ought to be translatable into an immanent culture. The question then is what does this look like, and how does this translation occur? This is one of the many questions theopoetics is attempting to answer.

---

40. Vahanian, *Theopoetics of the Word*, 15.

41. Ibid.

42. Ibid.

# Chapter 2

# Questions

*This is the only theological theme. Theology is an exercise about the marriage of Word and flesh, an endless poem about the mystery of the incarnation. Words and flesh make love and the body is born . . .*
*Word and flesh,*
*without separation,*
*without confusion,*
*and yet*
*one single body.*[1]

—RUBEM ALVES

THE CONTEXT ARTICULATED IN the previous section provokes and invokes a number of questions; questions that those writing theopoetics ask and to which they offer theopoetics as an answer. Here I ask some of these questions alongside the community of theopoets, and in the following section I map out how different streams of thought were led, by similar questions, to theopoetics. Often this leading by the questions is not explicitly stated nor explicitly answered since both the call and the response occur gradually. Here I ask six questions—six: an incomplete number—that spur on theopoetic writers.

*How do we move forward?* Time presses all clocks forward, and the ruin of the early twentieth century makes the collective *we* wish that

1. Alves, *The Poet, the Warrior, the Prophet*, 75.

we could turn back time. But even if we could, would we truly take the chance of having to go through what seemed like the nadir of human existence again? With such horror in the recent past our gaze turns forward, but the forward gaze seems even more unpredictable! We are soft sift, pressed, squeezed forward and down by time; we are too small to stop the flow, and no matter how hard we dig our heals in, we cannot slow down.[2] We no longer run forward with open arms because the future may contain unimagined horrors. Nor do we make love to the past, for ghosts are hidden there just behind the veil of our memory. We are caught, trapped, and captured within the ever present now—seemingly incapable of optimism directed toward the future and repulsed by the past.

The narrative of progress, paradoxically only aggravates our existential dilemma. The cosmological and scientific revolutions are beginning to work their way deep into the human psyche. We have lost our center. Moreover, from special relativity to quantum mechanics we appear to know more than ever, but this has not alleviated our anxieties. Wilder captures this sentiment aptly, "Reality has become dizzying and uncharted but every particular contact with it all the more fresh and unpredictable. Thus the revolution in cosmology has shocked not only our intellectual but also our imaginative categories."[3] We are more aware that we, as a species, are moving into uncharted waters with great unknowns that loom just beyond the horizon. These unknowns are absent, but their absence is felt as a presence since we are never sure if anything is truly lurking just beyond the veil of the future. It is into this context that Wilder makes a massive claim. In relation to questions of ecology and exploitation of nature, some of those most looming present absences, he writes, "It is only through a theopoetic that these contemporary issues can be rightly explored."[4] Understanding the magnitude of his proposal, Wilder moves into the future not with naïve optimism, but with a necessary resolve.

*Who am I?* In a time of transit and transience, humanity's existential questions are ripped from their locations. All substance melts away into motion, and so too our platforms morph into train tracks. The *I*—the

---

2. I am indebted to Gerard Manley Hopkins for this wonderful image of time as the pressure upon the sand in an hourglass as well as the alliteration of "soft sift," both of which come from his prolonged poetic-theological reflection in "The Wreck of the Deutschland." Hopkins, *Major Works*, 111.

3. Wilder, *Theopoetic*, 4.

4. Ibid., 5.

ego—seems to move too quickly to be grasped. The *am* of being is no longer stable, no longer located, no longer grounded on granite. Instead we have chipped away at idols made of stone until it seems like nothing stable is left from which to push off—so now we drift away into space. Wilder again captures what these developments mean for the self. He writes, "For one thing appeal to the past becomes a problem when there is so much emphasis on iconoclasm and improvisation. 'I must invent myself,' is a recurrent motif. This [is a] dethroning of old authorities and worlds of meaning."[5] What was rock—old authorities—has dissolved, and we are now continually on the move, inventing ourselves in relation only to movement.

*Can humans communicate with the divine?* Is there even something ultimate with which to relate? Is there a last bastion of relation? From the tick-tock of the clock, to the choo-choo of the train, we have covered over the acts of the divine. From the sending of rain, to the regularity of the seasons, to the power of motion, we have attempted to master and control the world around them—and in many ways we have succeeded. But something remains unsaid. There looms a desire to say more. Regarding this desire and the human response Wilder writes, "We speak about a theopoetic because the theme of divinity requires a dynamic and dramatic speech. Divinity has to do with the glory of God and the creature's participation in it. But this means participation in his life and activity and this is something other than passive mystical illumination or epiphanies of the sacred."[6] Rather than being annihilated by an ultimate, there seems to be a soft call to speech. It is a call to participate in the questions through a response, and in so doing we appear to move from master to being mastered, from locutor to the interlocutor. In this moment we find ourselves relativized, made small, yet not solely in a negative way. The anxieties we accumulated due to our mastering of the world have shackled us with new chains for which we do not have the key. But as we are made small, perhaps the shackles will not seem so tight, and maybe they will even slip from our extremities. If there is a call that can make us small, then even a still small voice may be stronger than iron. However, answering the *how* when one finds oneself in a place to respond is still a further question.

5. Ibid., 34.
6. Ibid., 12.

*How are humans participants in communication?* Wilder's quote above advocates for an active response, an active participation. In relation to the divine, or a God who has spoken, the question of what form of activity or role the human plays in communication remains a very open question. For alongside and after the horrors of the early twentieth century was a movement toward relocating the reader into a more active role in relation to the text. Things spoken need to be heard; things written need to be read; or as the saying goes, "It takes two to tango." Therefore, from Gadamer's "merging of horizons,"[7] to Paul Ricoeur's "surplus of meaning,"[8] the trend toward dialogue over and against monologue within the expanding field of reader-response criticism is evident, as the reader's action and experiences are incorporated more openly into interpretation. This trend has achieved enough interpretive openness that feminist, queer, and post-colonial critics have been able to fight their way into the fray. Together these developments have fruitfully united with a reaction against hyper-cognitive existence thereby leading toward recognition of embodied knowing, wherein the entire human participates bodily in communication, not merely cognitively.[9]

7. "Every experience has implicit horizons of before and after, and finally fuses with the continuum of the experiences present in the before and after to form a unified flow of experience." Gadamer, *Truth and Method*, 246.

8. "Symbolic signification, therefore, is so constituted that we can only attain the secondary signification by way of the primary signification, where this primary signification is the sole means of access to the surplus of meaning." Ricoeur, *Interpretation Theory*, 55.

9. NB: Here I am aligning myself quite directly with one of two trends that have been developing and intermingling over the past two centuries. While there has been a trend toward more embodied ways of knowing, speaking, and relating as humans— which I highlight—both with each other and with our ecosystems, there has also been the dialectically opposing trend of hyper-individualism and isolation. This opposing trend, in my assessment, has led toward transhumanism in various forms such as posthumanism and technophilia—many expressions of which actively seek the supersession of the embodied human, sometimes by way of uploading consciousness to technological devices. These individualist directions of development often appear to value the cognitive world of humans over the physical and relational reality of humans. I find the direction that transhumanism takes to be an unhelpful reduction of humanity to mere mind, as opposed to a complex synthesis of mind and body—a reduction that I would in part trace back to the role and supremacy that the Cartesian subject has taken on in the Western world. By viewing the two trends as a dialectic, I desire to affirm individuality but not at the expense of physicality and relations. As such, I focus here on the relational and embodied aspects of communication, which I think can actively include and inform a robust individuality without leading to escapist and reductionist thinking. For more on challenging hyper-cognitive, or hyper-spiritual,

*What do humans need to be freed from?* If the divine, specifically the Christian God, speaks a word of freedom, then we need to ask this question. The question im*plies* we are slaves to something and need liberation from it. For Alves, in the Global South, and many others who move in a theopoetic direction, it is western European cognitive structures that have become the oppressor. Caputo highlights this when he writes that we must address "the sociology which is everywhere around us today, which instantiates the binary oppositional schemes of Western metaphysics: higher and lower, ruler and ruled, cause and effect, science and opinion, master and slave, same and different, male and female, rich and poor, privileged and unprivileged."[10] The binaries that previously ordered our thoughts, our societies, and our existence have become the oppressor, and it is from these chains we must break free.

*How do we engage power?* Awareness of discourses of power, specifically humanity's ability to speak about them openly, has exploded onto the intellectual landscape in the late twentieth and early twenty-first centuries. Religion's ability to converse within this new landscape will shape its relevance in the foreseeable future. Within the theopoetic discourse there appears to be an awareness of what is at stake. For example, Alves powerfully describes the close relation between what is commonly thought of as religion and discourses of power: "The end of religion? No. The advent of a new religion. Power now takes the place of religion as it promises to fulfill its dreams."[11] Thus Alves sees power as the new religion in that power seeks to actualize the promises of religion. Whereas the church and religious belief previously were the loci of hope for a better life, now economic and political power in secularized forms have become the main arbiters of power in terms of actualizing the desires of the populace—and their function in realizing hopes and promises then takes on a religious role in society. Moreover, Caputo, aligning with Derrida, locates his engagement within this question of power thus:

> Like [Michel] Foucault, like a good many philosophers today, Derrida is concerned with power, its effects, its use and abuse, its delimination. He is interested in what he calls the *pouvoir-écrire*, the power of writing, writing power, the discourse of power and the power of discourse, its capacity to exclude, to declare abnormal, to repress, to standardize, to devalorize and

existence, see the section on Rubem Alves in chapter 3.

10. Caputo, *Radical Hermeneutics*, 260.
11. Alves, *The Poet, the Warrior, the Prophet*, 109.

> degrade. The work of deconstructive analysis is aimed at con-
> centrations of power which are above all the targets of decenter-
> ing and dissemination.[12]

Rather than fleeing from discussions of power, both Alves and Caputo foray into discourses of power, with the intent of critiquing, fracturing, and attempting to decenter and disseminate potentially oppressive discourses. As such, theopoetics informed by these authors gains relevance because it understands and antagonizes the shifting structures of power thereby weakening the idolatrous roles these structures assume.

---

12. Caputo, *Radical Hermeneutics*, 193.

# Chapter 3

# The Folds: A Braided River
# of Theopoetics

*I would like to become unfamiliar with everything*
*in order to see again*
*to hear again*
*to feel again.*[1]

—RUBEM ALVES

IT APPEARS TO BE a recurrent story in the late twentieth century for an academician to arrive at the term theopoetics, seemingly independent of one another, only to find out later that Stanley Hopper had already coined the term *theopoiesis*. Both Wilder and Keller openly recount such stories.[2] I would like to offer two initial thoughts regarding these independent, yet reoccurring, accounts of arriving at overlapping conclusions. First, as I have begun to argue up until this point, the cultural milieu widely experienced in Western society in the late twentieth century seems to incline various thinkers to consider poetics and theopoetics. Those who find themselves led to theopoetics often articulate their journey in this direction as a response to sterile forms of language or a personal development due to their own awareness of their cultural situatedness and

1. Alves, *The Poet, the Warrior, the Prophet*, 18.
2. Wilder, *Theopoetic*, iv; Keller, *Cloud of the Impossible*, 369n10.

the affects this then has on their understanding of language, often with respect to language's relation to the divine. In this section I will argue that while individuals follow various trajectories toward theopoetics—each a distinct and recognizably different path with unique influences and history—they are not mutually exclusive. Second, and more specific than a broad cultural disposition, the stories of Wilder and Keller coming to the term *theopoetics* without awareness of its previous origin speak in part, at least, to the influential and lasting—but apparently nearly unconscious—imaginarium developed and maintained within Drew and Syracuse Universities. Hopper, Vahanian, Caputo, and Keller have all taught in these institutions, and Wilder and many others encountered their thought.[3] Keller, herself, traces theopoetics in this specific context back to a series of conferences at Drew University in 1962, 1964, and 1966, which occurred, as David Miller states, "at the intersection of left-wing Bultmannian biblical interpretation, the thought of the late period of Heidegger's existential phenomenology, and the Religion and Literature movement."[4] This diversity, that is an integral part of the origin of theopoetics, is a lasting illustration of how theopoetics is generated and flourishes at the confluence of various streams of thought. Once this generative locale, inclusive of diversity, is recognized—by way of identifying a specific location that promoted interdisciplinary conversations—and when melded with the broader societal context that was leading individuals to ask similar questions, a generous spring is revealed. These two forces begin to form an initial explanation as to why what at first glance may appear to be apparently separate streams of thought, academicians, and multiple discourses all flow—as though guided by an unseen gravity—toward theopoetics.

The ensuing river of theopoetics can be imagined as three distinct streams flowing through a large delta.[5] These streams meander through

---

3. Wilder, *Theopoetic*, iv.

4. Keller, "Theopoiesis and the Pluriverse," 184; Miller, "Theopoetry or Theopoetics?," 9.

5. While I here focus on the lineages, persons, and different influence as a means to map the discourse, Harrity parses the discourse differently by highlighting three modes that theopoetics takes on which "bleed into one another." They are: "1. *The Corporeal Mode* arrays creaturely experience and human interaction, aiming to maintain and reflect existential nature with nuance and complex variety. 2. *The Prophetic Mode* bears witness to and provides a clear vision of the way people value landscapes, resources, personhood, and dignity, both human and divine. 3. *The Mystical Mode* seeks to engage a transcendent and contemplative divine intelligence that is both within and

one another, sometimes appearing to be one stream, sometimes two, and occasionally splitting into three discrete streams. As a braided river, the currents within these streams, though unique, flow together, reinforcing one another, crossing over one another, and even causing eddies and pools of apparent calm as they draw us—the reader, the writer, the listener, and the poet—out to sea, into the open abyss, and toward the great unknown.

I hope to show that within these streams, the river, and the sea beyond, there are places to relax and dream, areas of deadly rapids, unfathomable depths, and fresh water that quench thirsts and wet the parched lips of the foreigner, the stranger, and the widow.[6] As I go about exploring the scope, width, currents, and headwaters of these folded streams, I also swim into the depths of this river, plunging into the theopoetic fold that descends below metaphysics, where the channel increases to seemingly ineffable depths. Yet without finding, claiming, or hitting rock bottom, I encounter the other side of the channel and begin to rise up the opposing bank toward the third stream, only to find myself drawn up into a watery cloud.

Before the water begins to churn too rapidly, I will note some guiding features in all three streams, so that you, the reader, can pay attention to how the currents in each of the three streams are unique and progress or respond slightly differently. Some of the common and influential topographical features that channel the river are an openness to the future, priority of embodiment, serious theological reflection based on the natural world, a concern for the oppressed, and the contingency of all things—even at points the contingency of God's very self and God's ontological existence.

## 3.1—IMAGINATION, THE DEATH OF GOD, AND LIBERATION: THEOPOETIC CURRENTS

The first stream of the threefold braided river has within it three identifiable currents. This stream flows from the originating source of

---

without embodiment." I mention these three here to acknowledge that there are many ways of categorizing the diversity within the discourse, and each casts its own light on what is going on within theopoetics; see Harrity, "Theopoetics of Literature," 12–13.

6. Alternatively stated: "Upon approaching the waters of theopoetics, one must be comfortable with the vulgarities of getting wet, the mists of liminality and the ripples of limbo." Harrity et al., "Theopoetics of Literature," 10.

theopoetics, where it babbles forth at the convergence of discourses. From this spring gush influential currents that guide the flow, or at least significantly influence the course of the latter two streams that join and weave through each other in the play of the river.

### 3.1.1—A Linguistic, Aesthetic Imagination: Refreshing Dreams

*Stanley Hopper*

Hopper stands at the headwaters of the theopoetic river. Hopper first used the term *theopoetics* in his 1971 American Academy of Religion address, "The Literary Imagination and the Doing of Theology."[7] A brief summary of this address will assist in understanding the convergence that precipitates the spring and the subsequent currents in the river. In his address Hopper begins by aligning himself with Heidegger by claiming that onto-theological assertions are highly questionable, which means one ought to realize that one is making representational statements when speaking of God.[8] With this idea of representation he is able to connect the doing/making/forming of theology to poiesis, which he identifies as the poetry of Being. For Hopper, a criterion for poetry is that poetry's metaphors must be current so that they can move—have *doing* power, an agency within—the reader or listener, but this does not always occur because some people may be resistant to updating or altering language.[9] However, while humanity may fail in this renewing of language, he argues, "The imagination goes deeper, soliciting the carrying power of the archetype, translating the archetype from the spent symbolic system into fresh embodiments."[10] Hopper here means that humanity's failure does not kill the power of metaphors; rather, they will arise through the imagination in a different form due to the power of the archetype. Consequently, Hopper is willing to let go of old symbols in order to make way for new manifestations of the archetype. For Hopper, "What this means is that 'God' (or, in Eastern thought, the realm of 'absolute emptiness') is in the realm beyond our conceptualistic dichotomies, and beyond our

---

7. Keefe-Perry, *Way to Water*, 17.

8. Hopper, *The Way of Transfiguration*, 207.

9. Ibid., 208–14.

10. Ibid., 220.

symbolic representations."[11] Theopoetics is then a making, or a forming, of *God* from this realm beyond conception. Hopper concludes with four points that sum up why he has arrived at this understanding of humanity's God-talk. He writes:

> We have proposed four things:
>
> 1) that our topology of being has changed [i.e., Heidegger];
>
> 2) that the Western consciousness is being transformed [i.e., changing metaphors and symbols];
>
> 3) that what matters in interpretation is the psychic depth which our modalities of identification through the imagination achieve; and
>
> 4) that our theo-logoi belong to the realm of mytho-poetic utterances and that theo-logos is not theologic but theo-poiesis.[12]

This suggestion by Hopper of a direction that God-talk should take in a world aware of the shortfalls of onto-theology may be seen as a significant departure from reflections about God common to the laity, but perhaps it is not an earth-shattering withdrawal from the flows and currents hidden within the history of Christian thought. For Hopper's understanding of *depth* and *archetype* that reconstitute in new metaphors, alongside his affirmation of a mytho-poetic, may hum a harmonious (though not identical) tune to that sung by the mystics and some of the apophatic tradition within Christianity.

As is evident, Hopper was seeking to articulate much more than the prettying up of theology to match an aesthetic whim. Rather he was offering a re-conception of how language relates to the divine. Keefe-Perry summarizes it this way, "[Hopper] did not understand the turn to the poetic as merely a superficial stylistic preference, but rather as a deep aesthetic recalibration in which the terms of discussion would be reconfigured to shift from a kind of scientific mechanicalism toward an organic and embodied surplus of meaning."[13] This appears to lead Hopper to the position, as explained by Keefe-Perry, "that our experience of God is not the Godhead-itself, but our filtered, human intuition."[14] Such an under-

---

11. Ibid., 221.
12. Ibid., 225.
13. Keefe-Perry, *Way to Water*, 28.
14. Ibid., 29.

standing leads, for many, to the conclusion that there is no such *thing* as God, but *God* is something that is *done* by human representational statements.

Hopper's recalibration of God-talk was complex and is helpfully explained in the preface to *The Way of Transfiguration*, a collection of his writings. The intellectual framework with which Hopper is working is a convergence of four modes of reflection: "theological, poetic, philosophical, and psychological—[which] he [Hopper] speaks of [as] a 'step back' from the dualistic, objective framework of Western thought; a 'step down' that shatters the rigid boundaries of the Western ego self; and a 'step through' that discovers the power of symbol and metaphor to open us to the divine not as supernatural object but as indwelling Presence and Mysterious Depth."[15] These three steps guide Hopper's work and form the basis of his critiques of diverse strands of Western thought and analysis, specifically its tendency toward reductionism. For example, in the introduction to *The Way of Transfiguration* Melvin Keiser notes how Hopper's motivation to inquire into the depth of existence (one of the three steps) was used by Hopper as a reason to critique both "Barth and the neo-orthodox revolution" and "theology of history" because both did not sufficiently engage with "the deep self and divine presence."[16] This critique illustrates that rather than merely switching terms, Hopper's theopoiesis arises from a robust meditation on the world, which supplies him with intellectual and theological power to critique both theologies that reduce *up* and become too high and transcendental as well as theologies that reduce *down* and make everything subject to the linearity of chronological time and limited to the surface of appearances.

As mentioned above, Hopper's thought developed at the nexus of various discourses in the mid-twentieth century, which in turn prompted a number of specific questions. Keefe-Perry highlights three questions from the third consultation on hermeneutics at Drew University (1966) that assist in understanding Hopper's intellectual queries. The questions are:

(1) What is the nature of the referent of the theological utterance? Or, what are we talking about when we talk about God?

---

15. Hopper, *The Way of Transfiguration*, vii.
16. Ibid., 9.

(2) What is the nature of thinking that is objectifying? Or, can we actually think anything without categorizing it, and how can we know categorizing is not just projecting?

(3) Is a non-objectivizing thinking and speaking possible? Or, if we can know the content of the second question can we speak about a thing without only speaking about an abstraction of it?[17]

Thus the focus of the conference was on whether a prelinguistic encounter with the world and the divine was possible and how to go about prioritizing the existential *now* over and against either a temporal past or temporal future. In this context poiesis as becoming in the present, as opposed to logos as being, came to be preferred as a way of understanding and answering these questions.[18]

Finally, Keefe-Perry sums up Hopper's influence on theopoetics this way. Hopper offered "an assertion that theopoetics is that which leads us into a new language where theologies are not rigid, logical assertions, but ecstatic expressions that plunge us into an experience of mystery and a primal being."[19] As such, the theopoetic river continues to be influenced by the fourfold currents Hopper set in motion insofar as theopoetics (1) prioritizes becoming; (2) is involved in the creation of new language, symbols, metaphors, and expressions; (3) continues to plumb the depths of mystery; and (4) is still wresting with the meaning of being.

### Amos Wilder

Wilder broadens, deepens, and guides the theopoetic stream begun by Hopper. In addition to assessing the location from which the spring poured forth (as discussed in chapter 1), Wilder is influential in the renewal and reincorporation of imagination and aesthetics into a religious mythology.[20] Following Hopper's lead, Wilder focuses on relevant language and argues that a recovery of the sacred requires the proper

---

17. Keefe-Perry, *Way to Water*, 20.

18. Keller quotes a definition by Hopper that highlights this focus on the existential *now*: "What theo-poiesis does is to effect disclosure through the crucial nexus of event, thereby making the crux of knowing, both morally and aesthetically, radically decisive in time." Keller, "Theopoiesis and the Pluriverse," 184.

19. Keefe-Perry, *Way to Water*, 30.

20. Wilder, *Theopoetic*.

vehicles of the symbolic and the imagination.[21] Therefore, rather than seeing symbolism and a mythical consciousness as "a loss of nerve or a repudiation of our best Western humanism we may rather find them signaling a return to the proper plenitude and diversity of our human nature as common to many epochs and climes."[22] Moreover, he argues, "What is needed today is more correlation of all such findings with our older traditions."[23] Essentially, he understands the culture of the seventies as longing for a renewal of the religious imagination; he claims that this longing for religious imagination is witnessed in that "depth is again calling to depth."[24] This cultural moment, for Wilder, is understood as an opportunity insofar as he perceives it to "augur a new age of faith. . . . [And to be] a big step beyond the 'death of God' even if it falls short of a more total vision."[25] As such, Wilder thinks the thirst of the culture's imagination might be quenched by the spring of theopoetics.

Wilder, attuned to his cultural context, also implores that theopoetics cannot be merely spiritualized fantasy or escapism but must be socially relevant and engaged. For "it is in this order of imagination and social dream . . . that we find the bridge between the theologian and action in his time, between theology and politics."[26] This nexus, identified by Wilder, of imagination, social dream, action, theology, and politics is precisely the locale into which authors like Walter Brueggemann wrote books such as *The Prophetic Imagination* (1978). While Brueggemann pioneered this thought in relation to the Hebrew Bible, Wilder was already in 1970 writing about the New Testament and social imagination. He describes the apostolic Scriptures as an imaginative "guerrilla operation which undermined social authority by profound persuasions. What no overt force could do it did by spiritual subversion at the level of social imagination of the polis and the provinces of the empire. It was a case of liturgy against liturgy, of myth against myth."[27] This robust assertion

21. Ibid., 13.

22. Ibid., 16.

23. Ibid., 21.

24. Ibid.

25. Ibid., 23.

26. Ibid., 27.

27. Ibid., 28. Also in this climate of socially engaged, imaginative biblical interpretation, Ched Myers takes up and applies the idea of a "War of Myth" in his landmark commentary on the Gospel of Mark (1988), which integrates a number of the concerns Wilder identifies as forming the theopoetic nexus; see Myers, *Binding The Strong*

of competing myths acts twofold: as both an explanation of how to understand the Scriptures and the means by which the theopoet becomes actively politically engaged and socially relevant in his or her own time.

Further developing his case for a theopoetic/mythopoetic imagination, Wilder argues in favor of theopoetic knowing rather than object thinking. Against object reductionism, he argues, "We are often instructed as to the intellectual and scientific revolution in our period. We also know about social and economic changes. But here we are interested in more elusive features of the situation: the reality-sense, the governing apperceptions, the sensorium."[28] He goes on, "At a more sophisticated if not more fundamental level we note in the field of philosophy the revolt against metaphysics, against 'objective thinking'—with Heidegger a return beyond Plato and Aristotle to the pre-Socratics, to the authentic wisdom of Being, or with existentialism generally, a focus on reality in terms of freedom and intentionality of a deeper self."[29] This move toward a deeper self can be understood as a move away from abstraction and toward the physical world and an imaginative engagement with it.

Finally, Wilder unites these aspects of his thought in what he calls "a mythopoetic." He states, "One cannot plead for a theopoetic without also defending a mythopoetic."[30] Wilder's mythopoetic includes an expansive, active, and seriously considered definition of myth: "One can at least begin by thinking in terms of social imagination and its myths and scenarios. I only insist that these involve the will as well as the dream. Our visions, stories, and utopias are not only aesthetic: they engage us. They also represent some kind of knowing as well as fancying. Myths, dreams, and imaginations are serious."[31] Thus Wilder reinforces nonreductionism as an aspect necessary for theopoetics by positing an expansive mythic understanding of the world in which a theopoetic can participate.

Therefore, one can sum up Wilder's contribution to theopoetics as adding to Hopper's three steps by guiding the theopoetic stream to include more pointedly the social imagination, the human will, cultural context, and social engagement. Wilder supports and empowers these

*Man*, 14–21.

28. Wilder, *Theopoetic*, 30.

29. Ibid., 31.

30. Ibid., 73. This is a position that many other writers of theopoetics would surely want to challenge; see the Caputo section below.

31. Ibid., 79.

aspects of theopoetics through his plea to return to a mythic religious imagination, which he thinks will continue to feed the renewed manifestations—the theopoetic river.

### 3.1.2—(Post)Death of God: Solid, Liquid, or Gas?

Death of God (DoG) theology—itself a diverse and multifaceted movement, a full discussion of which is beyond the scope of this work—has had a notable influence on theopoetics, and therefore it is worth considering this influential current of the stream that plays within the braided river of theopoetics.[32] DoG theology, as used in this book, refers to the theological movement begun in the 1960s within American theological circles. Keefe-Perry highlights that DoG or the "Radical Theology movement" was one of three key "circles of dialogue" in which Hopper was participating when he originated the term theopoetics; the other two being the "Society for the Arts, Religion, and Contemporary Culture; [and] Drew University's Consultations on Hermeneutics."[33] I will here consider one intellectual of the DoG movement whose work became specifically intertwined with theopoetics. As such, I hope that you, the reader, will be able to feel the force and power of the water moving within this DoG current and the direction it flows in a post-DoG variant.[34] This current, however, is a somewhat elusive flow as the stream seems solid at first, yet it dissipates and eventually melts into air.[35]

32. Keefe-Perry helpfully defines three streams of DoG theology: "(1) Thomas J. J. Altizer's 'extreme kenosis' theological argument, in which he posits 'God had become fully human in Christ, so as to lose his divine attributes and therefore his divine existence'; (2) William Hamilton's sociological argument 'that modern people were unable anymore to believe in God, and the church ought, therefore, to seek to do without him as well'; and (3) Paul Van Buren's social-linguistic claim that 'the concept of God was 'cognitively meaningless,' since God's existence and nature were not verifiable or falsifiable by the methods of science.'" Keefe-Perry, *Way to Water*, 23.

33. Ibid., 17.

34. Vahanian was deeply involved in the DoG conversations that were occurring in the 1960s, and these developments in theological thought significantly influenced his thought. However, Vanhanian continued to produce theology and theopoetics in the decades that followed; as such, his later work is *post-DoG* in that he is shaped and influenced by DoG theology, yet he continues to write after the DoG conversations, and his writings respond to and move beyond those developments.

35. "All that is solid melts into air, all that is holy is profaned, and man is at last compelled to face with sober senses, his real conditions of life, and his relations with his kind." *Marx-Engels Reader*, 476.

## Gabriel Vahanian

*The Death of God*, 1961, was a notable work in the DoG movement authored by Vahanian. In it Vahanian means the "death of God" primarily as a sociological statement in that the secularizing culture has lost a sense of transcendence as classically conceived; therefore, God has died (not killed per se, which would require a killer, nor nonexistent, which would necessarily be an ontological or metaphysical statement).[36] This articulation by Vahanian echoes Nietzsche's expression of "God is dead,"[37] which also primarily expresses a sociological articulation because Nietzsche's own eschewing of metaphysics prevents him from making such metaphysical claims (even if his sociological assessment would lead the reader by deduction to the conclusion that God is metaphysically dead, or nonexistent).[38]

Vahanian begins his work by addressing his reflection not to a metaphysically dead God but a practically (functionally) dead God. The way forward for Vahanian, then, is to reinvest God, as a word, with all the power of words in shaping the worlds (the cognitive makeup, description, and formation of human reality) of humanity as a practical (functional) response.[39] Vahanian's assertion of God as Word is not novel within the Christian tradition, but situated after the DoG, there is not necessarily a metaphysical correlate attached to the word *God*. Such an understanding may sound strange, and patience is most certainly required to understand the importance, thrust, and force of his position, which is an astute response to the critiques of religion in the late nineteenth and early twentieth centuries.

36. Vahanian, *Theopoetics of the Word*, 13–15.

37. The first occurrence in Nietzsche's writings of "God is dead" is in *The Gay Science*, 108: "*New struggles.* —After Buddha was dead, his shadow was still shown for centuries in a cave—a tremendous, gruesome shadow. God is dead; but given the way of men, there may still be caves for thousands of years in which his shadow will be shown. And we—we still have to vanquish his shadow, too." The more famous articulation of "God is dead" occurs in *The Gay Science*, 125; *Nietzsche Reader*, 219, 224.

38. This strand of thinking is distinguished from a parallel, and often complementary, strand of "God is dead" thought which traces its origins back to a Hegelian metaphysic of Spirit actualizing itself in materiality until it reaches completion in the incarnation: "God is realized as Subject, and as manifested Subjectivity is exclusively One Individual" (Hegel, *Philosophy of History*, 325–26). Others then take this beyond Hegel himself to claim that God has metaphysically died, and therefore "God is dead."

39. Vahanian, *Theopoetics of the Word*, 25–26.

Noëlle Vahanian, in the foreword to her father's posthumously published work *Theopoetics of the Word*, writes, "God is a nameless God; anonymous, God is the Word; made flesh, God is my vocation, not because I am Christian rather than Pagan, but because I am *tout court* [without addition or qualification]. Not because this is my God and not yours, but because God is language."[40] This excerpt is helpful in reframing Vahanian's theology after the DoG in that God is more directly tied with language, however, not merely identified with it. Thus transcendence is re-inscribed to refer to the "kenotic utopianism of language."[41] For "in language, even the impossible is possible" (echoes of Derrida), and "*language allows us to transcend the parochialism of our facticity.*"[42] Thus, God the Word comes to bear on the words of humanity, words that create worlds and make the impossible possible.

Vahanian, himself, plays with the phrase, "Wording the World and Worlding the Word," through which he attempts to open a third "Christo-morphic" space, between the theomorphic and the anthropomorphic.[43] This space attempts to split between what Vahanian sees as faith's most common pretensions: a reductionist binary of being either too "meta-physically (or biophysiologically) oriented or too spiritualistically (or mystically) oriented."[44] Vahanian, instead of choosing one or the other, perceives the space between these two poles as the more pregnant, con-tingent, and fruitful location.

This christological focus is very similar to Barth. Somewhat ironi-cally, however, in the same way Barth used it to free himself from Calvin and Aquinas, Vahanian is freeing himself from Barth. It is a "*corrective*" response that attempts to reframe the strength of Barth's transcendental move[45] in order to establish a more world-facing reality of the Word, which focuses not on *what* God is, but *that* God is.[46] Thus Vahanian's

---

40. Ibid., x.

41. Ibid., xi.

42. Ibid.

43. Ibid., xxi.

44. Ibid.

45. Barth's transcendental move is the in-breaking of—and distinction from—the wholly other, which can tend toward an a-historical faith relation to the transcendent *above*. Barth's usage of transcendence, however, is understood through the *analogia fidei* (analogy of faith) rather than the more classical conception of the move *above* through the *analogia entis* (analogy of being).

46. Vahanian, *Theopoetics of the Word*, 7–13, 32.

project attempts to translate Christianity, or what he calls "a biblical conception of God," into a cultural frame that is immanentist.[47] One might categorize Vahanian's project as theopoetics for a post-Christian world, as presenting a post-liberal understanding of Christianity wherein the language-game—a system of language, via Ludwig Wittgenstein, that has its own rules and grammar with meaning being derived from the use of language itself—continues to function for the Christian community. However, following Paul Tillich, Vahanian is not interested in a Christian ghettoized version of theopoetics but rather a secularizing vision that offers theopoetics to the culture as a whole.[48] Further, Vahanian views the Word becoming flesh as inherently iconoclastic in that it destroys metaphysical conceptions of God and speech about humanity because flesh becomes the indispensable access point to the divine, undermining abstract and detached conceptions of God, humanity, and the world. Therefore the only way forward is through theopoetics where the sign and the signified are not separate: God is a word, and humans are human in that they speak words that make worlds from a middle space.[49]

When initially considering the current of Vahanian's post-DoG theology one may be tempted to say it is *merely* a theology of language. However, Vahanian would probably make some quip that while God is language and that God is not more than language, God is also certainly not less than language. This double framing takes the reductionism out of the charge, for words are neither something, nor are they nothing.[50] The words ripple and move the water of the river, which means that language is "irreducible to either the real or the imaginary. And yet, stretching itself, it impels both of them till even they converge."[51] This is the mystery of the Word become flesh: that through the body the word acts as a bridge of language across a bankless river. This bridge spans the ineffable distance between identity/identification and difference, the one and

---

47. Ibid., 16.

48. Ibid., 130.

49. Ibid., 19. The word *God* shocks and challenges us to speak words. These words form our worlds (not earth—the earth goes around the sun while we, humanity, inhabit the world; worlds involve us). The formation of the worlds formed by our words happen *between* the flesh that speaks and the flesh that hears. Therefore, the world only exists insofar as it is in relation to a speaking and hearing of the words, and words, like the Word of God, are always enfleshing rather than abstracting for the world does not exist without the flesh.

50. Ibid., 35–52.

51. Ibid., 36.

the many, the same and the other.[52] This ability is the "Christomorphic" nature of language in that it spans the distance between, and constitutes both, oneself and the wholly other.[53]

Vahanian in many ways follows in the Protestant reformed-and-reforming tradition. He lays out a premise in the first lines of the chapter "Wording the World and Worlding the Word" that makes sense of his movement beyond a classical orthodoxy. He writes, "Polytheistic, monotheistic, or pantheistic, no system, including theism as well as atheism, ever dawns on the human imagination, that does not bear the seed of its own subversion."[54] As such, Vahanian's moving beyond classical theism is not so much a denial but a type of further affirmation of negation. This approach is similar to the classic articulation of Hegel's progressing dialectic—thesis, antithesis, and synthesis—that develops within time. But let me suggest that Vahanian is actually more closely allied to Slavoj Žižek's dialectic, which is a synthesis of Hegel and Lacan. In Žižek's version, the antithesis is *always already* a latent possibility within the thesis; therefore, the antithesis will inevitably deconstruct and challenge the thesis toward a new synthesis. Alternatively stated, insofar as a thesis is faithful to itself that same thesis will move beyond itself and thereby become no longer identical to its previous self.[55] This same sense of movement is implicit in Vahanian's premise, which therefore aligns itself more with a poiesis, as forming, than it does with a static *logos*. Vahanian conveys this progression of reformed-and-reforming powerfully in his introduction to the chapter "God and the Fallacy of Identity: A Theological Disintoxication of the West":

> Wording the world out,
> the Word is worlded
> And worded is the body
> that bodies forth the Word
> And the word becomes flesh

52. Ibid., 39.

53. Ibid., 41. The self, relationally understood, requires an *other* who is not the self in order to understand itself. This *other* is accessed through language/words and therefore spans the gap of relation. Thus the W/word is that which is able to connect and at the same time establish an insurmountable difference: identification without sameness and difference without division.

54. Ibid., 25.

55. Caputo, *The Insistence of God*, 118, 136–47; Žižek and Milbank, *The Monstrosity of Christ*. Rollins also develops a similar line of dialectical progression in *The Fidelity of Betrayal*.

Abram becomes Abraham, Jacob becomes Israel, and Saul becomes Paul. The God of Abraham is and is not the God of Israel, and the God of Israel is and is not that of Paul.[56]

Assessing Vahanian's theopotics is difficult, not only because it is challenging to articulate conceptually, but also in part because he is redefining so many terms and speaking of language by means of language. Nevertheless, an element of thankfulness and gratitude within his work should not be overlooked. Vahanian, through his Christomorphic centerpiece, highlights words as the gifts that enable worlds to be formed. Words are gifts that cannot be accounted for—gifts that indebt both the speaker and listener by way of an un-owned origin and an unasked-for receiving—but also language is a grace that enables forgiveness. For as words form worlds in which to live, one may form a Christomorphic identity in this formed context—all because words have freed the world.[57]

Finally, Vahanian's theopoetics responds to the very contextual situation he so astutely identified (see chapter 1)—that of translating Christianity into an immanent context. He argues, "Originally born of the liturgy, theology is and remains tied to a culture."[58] But, for Vahanian, this is not a problem because his fluid universal is language not concepts: "God is a matter of words. So is deconstruction a matter of language. Concepts come and go. Language hangs on its ability to transfer word from one tongue into another."[59] Thus the solid of flesh through the fluidity of language becomes the air of the word; and the air of the words flow together into language that forms the world that in turn worlds more words.

### 3.1.3—Liberation: Water for a Thirsty World

*Where will the world go to drink if all the springs have been sealed and all the streams damned? Where will the widow draw water if the wells of life run dry and hopes blow away like dust in a desert wind? Where will the stranger seek refuge if animals are reduced to bleached bones scorched by the sun? Where will the orphan seek solace when a tear is too precious to be shed? Where will the traveler eat when there is not enough water to*

56. Vahanian, *Theopoetics of the Word*, 53.

57. Ibid., 80–85.

58. Ibid., 127.

59. Ibid., 120.

*wash her feet? When the rich and the poor no longer share a table and a cup, will there still be a world? When words lack sustenance and stories no longer quench our thirsts, what will be left? Who will be able to stand in that barren wasteland?*

## *Rubem Alves*

Alves, of Brazil, is the most notable author in the liberation current of our theopoetic stream. As the first liberation theologian, Alves has uniquely shaped and highlighted the liberating power of theopoetics.[60] More recently Alves has been joined by others who are writing at the confluence of art, theology, and social action; of note is Matt Guynn whose two articles, "Theopoetics: That the Dead May Become Gardeners Again" and "Theopoetics and Social Change" take up a discussion regarding the importance of reviving the imagination for engaging in liberating movements.[61] However, here I will focus specifically on Alves and the journey that led him to theopoetics.

Multiple routes toward theopoetics are evident in Alves's life and work. Sergio de Gouvea Franco highlights one trajectory of change within Alves, noting that the concept of liberation "in his first works . . . is highly political (especially in his first two books). However, his concept of liberation moves smoothly into a more personal notion."[62] This move toward personal liberation loosely coincides intellectually and temporally with his turn toward theopoetics, which "is expressed [by Alves] as a deeply personal, therapeutic reorientation to the world."[63] Craig L.

60. Alves did his doctoral studies at Princeton Theological Seminary. His dissertation dealt with social and political concerns and was published under the name *A Theology of Human Hope* (1968)—originally titled *Toward a Theology of Liberation*, prior to editorial changes. As such, he was doing theology from a liberation perspective prior to Gustavo Gutierrez's *A Theology of Liberation* (1971); see De Gouvea Franco, "The Concepts of Liberation and Religion in the Work of Rubem Alves," 2–4.

61. Guynn, "Theopoetics: That the Dead May Become Gardeners Again"; Guynn, "Theopoetics and Social Change." This current also manifests in Keefe-Perry's writings. Of note is his essay "Toward the Heraldic."

62. De Gouvea Franco, "The Concepts of Liberation and Religion in the Work of Rubem Alves," 13.

63. Hocking, "Liberating Language," 15–16. Alves describes the change as a conversion, a result of his daughter's birth: "I broke with the academic style because I decided that life is very short, very mysterious, and I didn't have the time to waste with academics. I would only say things in the most honest manner. . . . This was a moment of true conversion" (16).

Nessan helpfully understands Alves's reorientation and frames this transition as Alves becoming an artist: "For centuries theologians, cerebral beings, had devoted themselves to transforming beauty into rational speech. Beauty was not enough for them. They wanted certainty, they wanted truth. However, artists, beings of the heart, know that the highest form of truth is beauty."[64] As Alves became a theopoet, he began to make use of beauty as discourse; and as a result "his writing clearly invites the in-breaking of the transcendent into the space-time coordinates of this world, yet without any desire to categorize or capture. His project is more aesthetic than discursive."[65] Yet while easy to summarize, the coinciding trajectories of social liberation developing into personal liberation and analytical argumentation budding into theopoetics took many decades to be fully realized in the life of Alves.

Alves's theopoetics did not arise out of a vacuum, nor solely out of a love for beauty; his work arose out of his Brazilian context and the oppression and repression occurring as a result of a certain form of dominating discourse. Alves's work *Protestantism and Repression* highlights the connections between Protestant discourse and the repression of the people of Brazil.[66] Mayers summarizes Alves's argument thus: "[Alves] claims that Protestantism is bad, Right-Doctrine Protestantism is worse, both are repressive within the Brazilian religious setting, and both are extremely dangerous within the world religious setting."[67] "Right-Doctrine Protestantism (RDP)" is a discourse and theology that "focuses on the anxieties of men and women unable to cope with the personal and sociological explanations for and solutions to . . . crises, this type of Protestantism attaches ontological significance to them. They [i.e., the crises] are spoken of theologically, in terms of sin, disobedience to God, guilt, etc. The answer offered is salvation through conversion."[68] Rather than deal with social and political problems, RDP relativizes and spiritualizes the issues in order to fit a preconceived theological matrix.

Having witnessed these spiritual narrativizations of events occurring around him, Alves identifies those indoctrinated by RDP as those reacting against movements of social and political change because they

---

64. Nessan, "Transparencies of Eternity," 59.
65. Ibid., 60.
66. Alves, *Protestantism and Repression*.
67. Mayers, "Protestantism and Repression," 249.
68. Alves, *Protestantism and Repression*, xiv.

see liberation elements as a betrayal of the gospel. This understanding of betrayal is theologically linked with an ontology of creation as stasis and sin as change. Therefore, any hope for change in material reality is linked to a sinful disposition. Alves's critique goes further, identifying RDP with the conservative element of the church; Richard Shaull summarizes his position, "Many middle-class lay men and women, whose whole system of values and way of life were called into question by what was happening in society at large, took refuge in a closed and absolute system, and supported those church leaders who provided such a system for them while using it for their own ends."[69] Thus RDP became a self-supporting system resistant to change by reinforcing the desires of safety, security, stability (the current *as is* structure of the world), and certainty.

Alves saw that the failure of Protestantism, specifically RDP, went much deeper than a conservative segment of the church with a propensity to hyper-spiritualize life to maintain the status quo. RDP, he thought, was bankrupt at the level of discourse. Alves's critique, as explained by Jeffrey Hocking, was that "the Brazilian Protestant church preferred to think of the meaning and life of the sign [i.e., the Bible] as self-sufficient and guaranteed. To suggest that a sign in itself is dead was interpreted as an attack on the universal verifiability of Christian doctrine."[70] In this context Alves followed Karl Barth in asserting that the sign/Bible needs to become alive in the reader/listener, rather than remaining complete and separate from humanity; metaphor needs to become enfleshed in a way unsuitable to a static text and scientific approach.[71] Alves satirizes the RDP position this way, "But we are modern. We have lost the grace of standing under that which we do not understand. Every mystery must be dissolved by our doing: we are justified by works."[72] Alves continues the ironic caricature, "We want the light of interpretation. Interpretation: the text is obscure. Our flashlights are needed. . . . Poets suffer from a linguistic disturbance. . . . This is why the interpreter is needed to save the poet from his verbal incompetence. Every poem must become scientific

---

69. Ibid., xii.

70. Hocking, "Liberating Language," 20.

71. Alves writes, "If we were sensitive to the metaphoric use of language we would have had visions of this mystery: the identity between word and body. But we, Protestants, are literalists. We are modern. We have moved away from the company of poets and magicians, in order to enter the world of science. And we have missed the point." Alves, "Theopoetics," 166.

72. Ibid.

discourse. Beauty must become knowledge."[73] Thus in his mockery of a sign-based approach to the text, Alves rejects onto-theo-logic theology[74] and analogical theology.[75] By rejecting these aspects of the Protestant (RDP) discourse, Alves implicitly creates criteria for a different discourse so that it does not fall into the same traps of hierarchy, stasis, oppression, and dehumanizing potential as the prior discourse.[76]

Alves understood this brand of Protestantism that he was rejecting as being pernicious and life denying. Regarding this Alves states, "The didactic concern has always been dear to the Protestant soul: pure hearts, clear ideas, logical thought. Action follows thought: this is the rule for all those who have been reached by saving grace."[77] The mechanical nature of this sequencing inevitably, for Alves, led to the reality that Protestant-ism was "dragged along to be nothing more than a secularized version of the Christian faith."[78] Attached to this worldview were many life-denying elements such as financial saving.[79] According to Alves, "In saving, the

73. Ibid., 167.

74. Guynn explains, "Onto-theo-logic, in which logic and rational 'truth' rises above the search for wisdom, asserts that we must accept or reject an asserted reality, at which point the writer's (preacher's, activist's) task is over. There is no invitation, mystery, or ambiguity of being, no point of entry or connection." Guynn, "Theopoet-ics: That the Dead May Become Gardeners Again," 100.

75. Hocking, "Liberating Language," 13. In these ways Alves responds not only to his Brazilian context but also to the larger Christian tradition, in which, as Hocking states, "it is no longer possible to assume that our language describes God by mak-ing analogous claims governed by a metaphysics of being. The fall of the analogical method is sure to be contested, but it is clear that speaking of God via analogy is no longer the default method in contemporary, Protestant theology." Hocking continues, "This is true even in some Catholic circles, led by figures such as John Caputo and Jean-Luc Marion."

76. Ibid., 14–36. Hocking also makes a compelling case that by moving away from the analogical method Alves offers a way toward a democratization of the language of faith. "The analogical method, governed by the principles of the Great Chain of Being, is implicitly hierarchal and exclusionary in both theological and societal expressions." Ibid., 18. As a result of the analogical method there are necessarily the *qualified* and *unqualified* groupings of those able to do theology proper, a conclusion Alves does not affirm.

77. Alves, "The Protestant Principle and Its Denial," 215.

78. Ibid.

79. Using a story of a dead man who floats ashore and is buried by the commu-nity, Alves writes, that before the dead man "their attitudes towards money could be described as dominated by the 'saving motif.' And for good reasons. Since they could not see any perspectives of change in the village, what they hoped for in the future was to move somewhere else. And this demanded money. So, they worked hard, lived very

present is emptied, it becomes only a *means* for something in the future; life is postponed. Spending, on the contrary, is possible only if one is not anxious about the future and committed to life in the present."[80] Alves's critique is that an overly clarified and moralistic Protestantism had become dead and was attempting to transplant itself into Brazil. "The presupposition was that Protestant theology had completed the codifying of biblical truths. The system of doctrine in harmony with the Scriptures was already perfected. Pastors may have studied theology, but the idea of an original theological production was inconceivable."[81] This dead church, Alves posited, would continue in the status quo so long as it remained anti-Roman and pro-growth because such a church would still retain an identity—hollow and ghostly as it may be—and be able support the parish and the pastor financially.[82] This type of static Protestantism was being forced to change, however, because of 1950s social-political movements and the growth of alternative ideas.[83] In this changing context, Protestantism would no longer hold the sole ideological position of being anti-Roman and pro-growth, thus Alves began putting forward a new way of doing theology. Reflecting on this new mode of theology Alves writes,

> I will say this that I think this model of doing theology is an erotic model. I no longer work with the category of truth. I don't know what truth is. But I know what is beautiful, I know what is good, I know what gives pleasure. I think that bodies are moved not by a conviction about truth, but by the seduction of the beautiful. I am developing this theology because I am interested in seeing people do things. And a theology based on epistemology, no

---

ascetic lives, spent only what was strictly necessary for survival, and saved what was left. This combination of hard work and asceticism created a particular ethos which even became the object of careful scientific study by Max Weber, a well known scientist who had been there in BD [before the dead man] times. Another philosopher who had visited the village even before, Karl Marx, came to similar conclusions, and noted that this ethos had the result of deforming the sensual life of people. The body ceased to be an *end*, it became a *means* for saving, and all the senses, which are the organs of pleasure, were repressed to the point of being suppressed." Alves, *The Poet, the Warrior, the Prophet*, 62–63.

80. Ibid., 63.

81. Alves, "The Protestant Principle and Its Denial," 218–19.

82. Ibid., 221.

83. Ibid., 224.

matter how fierce, doesn't move people. We are not constructed
in a Cartesian way. We are erotically constructed.[84]

His alternative vision of what theology must become in order to flourish in
his rapidly changing Brazilian context moved strongly away from dead and
dying dogmatically-held categories to find a new pulse in the body with all
its pleasures. As such, he was leaving the mechanistic model of modernity
in search of something else—perhaps we should call it *corpo-nity*, an era
conditioned by being embodied, in honor of his Brazilian body.

This movement was also toward theopoetics because Alves's understanding of Christ as poet-liberator—one who affirms life and enables
change—provokes him into a different mode of discourse that embodies
language that woos and erotically calls for a response through beauty,
goodness, and pleasure. Alves's liberationist slant of theopoetics has been
influential in terms of directing the discourse toward a *this-worldly* focus, one that involves bodies, desire, and physical existence. One might
even go so far as to consider Alves's *metaphysic* a body, or a *metaphysic* of
food.[85] For in an extended section on food and the body in a chapter entitled "Words Which Are Good to Be Eaten," Alves writes, "Reality is not
rawness, the 'things-in-themselves'. Reality is the result of the alchemic
transformation by fire, the food which is taken inside my body. Reality is
this encounter between mouth and food, desire and its object."[86] As such,
Alves's theopoetics deeply affirm all aspects of bodily existence as a form
of liberation from abstraction.

Through the journey of his life, his keen reflections, and living always with an eye toward the world and the oppressed, Alves became an
incredibly gifted theopoet. He is probably the most rhapsodic theopoet
considered in this book and to summarize his writing is to do violence
both to the beauty of his words and the nature of his project. Therefore,
instead of recounting more of his work in this section I have chosen to

---

84. Alves, "Eros, Language and Machismo: An Interview with Rubem Alves," 460.

85. It is extremely difficult to summarize Alves's theopoetic work without doing
significant violence to it, but Patrick Reyes provides a succinct and respectful attempt.
He writes, "Rubem A. Alves invites the reader in *The Poet, the Warrior, the Prophet*
to share a meal with him: a meal consisting of words that consume the party guests!
As Alves prepares and cooks the ingredients he tells his readers, his guests, a series of
stories, proverbs and reflections on a variety of topics such as epistemology, academia,
biblical studies, theology and poetry." Reyes, "Playing with Alves: In Memoriam," 87.

86. Alves, *The Poet, the Warrior, the Prophet*, 86.

pepper this entire book with his writing so that you might savor his delicious cuisine.

## 3.2—A PHENOMENOLOGICAL, HERMENEUTIC MOVEMENT: A FLOW WITHIN THE FLUX

Continental philosophy of religion is the second stream of the braided river investigated here, which weaves in and out of—influencing, and being influenced by—the other two streams as it makes its way out to sea. Within this stream, one might say, there are two intermingled currents that again mutually reinforce the flow: phenomenology and hermeneutics. In this section I will engage these currents by way of two contemporary thinkers: Caputo and Kearney, through their respective works *Radical Hermeneutics* and *The God Who May Be*. By way of these relatively recent works, written in the late twentieth and early twenty-first centuries, I will explore some of their particularities and draw connections to how the developments in phenomenology and hermeneutics flow toward theopoetics. In many ways I am beginning this downstream of many of the developments that lead to theopoetics, yet I do not intend to disregard earlier thinkers. Rather, by entering the current current I intend on revealing some of the figures and thoughts upstream that have set the water awhirl—those that now thrust us downstream into what is *to come*. As such, the influences of Derrida, Levinas, Ricoeur, Gadamer, Heidegger, Edmund Husserl, and even Søren Kierkegaard are felt in the current flow and aid in propelling the waters toward theopoetics.

### *John Caputo*

In many ways Caputo's 1987 work *Radical Hermeneutics* released a flood of potential energy that was building up behind metaphysical theological edifices which were coming under attack by philosophy, specifically phenomenological approaches of understanding being and knowing. The chipping away at the dam had begun long before Caputo's landmark work, but with it Caputo thrusts interpretation downstream into uncharted waters, further than many want to go. It is there, Caputo argues, beyond classical hermeneutics—into what is novel and new—that one will encounter events that are ever coming in the river but are always unforeseen. Here I will rearticulate the main developments within the text—developments that lead Caputo toward theopoetics—before discussing Caputo's particular theopoetics that seek the event to come.

Caputo, experiencing the flows and flux of his current moment, attempts to draw as near to the unpredictability of life as possible. He therefore chooses phenomenology and hermeneutics as the means to investigate life because these disciplines seek to stay close to experience. Hermeneutics, for Caputo, is "an attempt to stick with the original difficulty of life, and not to betray it with metaphysics."[87] It is this "difficulty of life," as guiding principle, that Caputo refuses to let go. He rebuffs any attempts to build *boats*, *docks*, or *bridges* that would extract him from the flow of life and all of its irregularities and difficulties. Building such extracting edifices would, in Caputo's opinion, only alienate one from life. With this in mind, he chooses to engage radical thinkers of the flux.

Caputo begins his inquiry with Kierkegaard and a distinction Kierkegaard formed under the pseudonym Constantin Constantius: the difference between "Greek recollection" and "Christian repetition."[88] Recollection is a backward movement—something lost is to be regained—(i.e., *exitus, reditus*), whereas repetition is a creative production forward (i.e., garden to garden-city). This distinction is the first of many that will become, by way of Derrida, a messianic focus on the "to come," which looks for the novel, the new, or the rupture through repetition. However, what is *new* in the flux of life does not come with certainty like a metaphysical structure, rather the *new* is more like life in that it is uncertain and therefore it provokes "fear and trembling . . . [and] the anxiety by which the existing individual is shaken."[89] Thus Caputo does not attempt to explain away the difficulty of life but rather intends on unmasking it, drawing near to it, and existentially experiencing it.

A key point in Caputo's argument is that repetition takes seriously a Christian conception of time. Rather than metaphysics, which "wants to think its way out of time," Christianity proposes that "every moment is literally momentous, an occasion for momentous choice," because "every moment of the Christian conception of time is touched by the eternal, has the eternal at stake, is charged with the energy and momentousness of an eternal—and that means a future—possibility."[90] Having criticized

---

87. Caputo, *Radical Hermeneutics*, 1.

88. Ibid., 2.

89. Ibid., 12.

90. Ibid., 15.

recollection by way of Kierkegaard, Caputo continues his metaphysical iconoclasm in tearing down Hegelian mediation that appears to affirm *kinesis* but does so only in a half-hearted way that abstracts the individual from the flow and flux of time.[91] Therefore, it is by way of Kierkegaard that Caputo casts off from all metaphysical moorages in order to fully embrace the flow of life. To briefly draw a connection, Caputo's project seeks in many ways the physicality and temporality of life, life without abstraction or reduction to mere cognition. Thus the goal of approaching life in his radical hermeneutics project—which eventually results in an explicit theopoetics—requires him to create an arena in which to think/write/be without abstraction, always already within an eternally charged moment of time.

Caputo continues to develop his radical hermeneutics as an affirmation of life by making his way through the phenomenological tradition seeking and destroying lapses into metaphysical thinking, lapses that would extract one from experiencing life, both phenomenologically and linguistically, as always something requiring interpretation. While appreciative of Husserl for analyzing the "internal time-consciousness" of the noetic subject, a project which mirrors Kierkegaard's more existential emphasis, Caputo argues that Husserl is guilty of fixing the flux in his understanding of "constitution" as an "anticipatory" movement that sketches out beforehand (predelineation) patterns (fore-structures) of what will come and thereby insulates phenomenology from the radical unpredictability of the flux.[92] Caputo is following Foucault's understanding that views the Husserlian self to be "two selves: one situated in the world and the other, its transcendental double."[93] This dual-self ultimately leads, in Caputo's opinion, to Husserl conceiving of interpretation as only arising from "a failure of absolute givenness," thereby entailing a desire to return to, or *recollect*, the lost origin rather than proceeding by way of repetition into the new.[94] This focus on recollecting an original meaning then directs interpretation by having a goal of *pinning-down* a meaning in the same way predelineation and fore-structures attempt to *harness* experiences in an anticipatory way, which, for Caputo, does not

91. Ibid., 17–21.
92. Ibid., 37–47.
93. Ibid., 57.
94. Ibid.

entail a sufficiently radical openness to the future and the unknown that is perhaps to come.

Caputo then, rejecting a dual-self and recollection, moves on to Heidegger whose hermeneutic sensibilities assist Caputo in flushing out these underlying presuppositions (fore-structures) postulated by Husserl. Heidegger lays out a hermeneutical circle that acknowledges one is always already entangled in such ontological fore-structures: fore-having, fore-sight, and fore-grasping.[95] This notion of one's existence as being *always already* entangled or engaged within fore-structures undercuts a notion that an anticipatory fore-structure might in some way add stability to one's interpretation of experience or a text. While this *always already* is useful because it places the individual again into the midst of experience, Caputo argues that Heidegger also adopts a form of recollection or circular movement in attempting to get back to ontological existence as *Dasein* since for Heidegger interpretation is simply understood as a return to the right presuppositions rather than a more Kierkegaardian linear movement.[96] Thus, for Caputo, even Heidegger does not achieve a vulnerable enough exposure to the flux of life, to the degree that he attempts to retrieve a place of stability. Within the noetic sense of knowing what is to come Heidegger posits circularity, a near-metaphysical assertion that assumes a circular movement exists into which one needs to enter correctly. In contrast, "repetition functions as a way of establishing identity and of coping with the flux, not as a way of denying it."[97] Resultant from this distinction is Caputo taking Heidegger beyond Heidegger, in that Caputo places Being in time so much so that there is not a certainty of what lies ahead. In other words, there is no guarantee that what is to come in one's experience, or for that matter interpretation, will be circular; it may be linear, spiral, or perhaps trapezoidal; but even beyond those it might be a wormhole or a black hole—who could say!

Caputo, continuing down the stream in search of a phenomenology and hermeneutics of life, then considers three directions hermeneutics takes after Heidegger's *Being and Time*—two of which he sees as arresting the flow of the flux, and one which is most faithful to the flux of life. First, Heidegger's later writings successfully dismantle the Cartesian subject, but the idea of a hermeneutical circle is neither radical nor metaphysically

95. Ibid., 53, 70.
96. Ibid., 60, 71.
97. Ibid., 92.

iconoclastic enough because a circle "still suggests a transcendental and methodological gesture, some kind of prior, subjective determination."[98] Second, regarding Gadamer's philosophical hermeneutics, Caputo assesses that Gadamer follows Hegel in putting forms into time and thereby allowing "a plurality of articulations of the same truth" but that the *true* is still external (metaphysical) in some respect.[99] While the eternal unchanging truth is not Gadamer's focus in *Truth and Method*, as Gadamer wants to focus on "how meaning and truth get passed along and handed down" thereby entertaining the flux by focusing on the transmission and genealogical aspects of truth, Caputo correctly identifies that Gadamer still assumes that something of truth remains exterior to the flow of time and transmission.[100]

Caputo finds what he thinks is the strongest current in Derrida and deconstruction. This current embraces repetition and the flux of life, and it is here that poetics emerge. Derrida seeks no moorage; he is willing to "put Being as presence into question, to uproot the desire of metaphysics to stabilize, ground and center beings in an onto-theological ordering, in a system of permanent presence."[101] Distinguishing between the "rabbi" and the "poet," Derrida proposes two routes of hermeneutics: one, of "a religious subordination to an original text and conceives itself as humble commentary, explication" a more *midrashic* approach; or, the other, of a poet "impudent and autonomous, an outlaw" that more closely resembles Peter's *pesher* interpretation in Acts.[102] One is bounded like an irrigation channel; the other rushes like a mountain stream in flood and is overflowing into discoveries of the new, or one might say that it exudes jubilant irrepressible openness to the Spirit—*Viens, oui, oui.*[103] Having found the current that keeps him most closely aligned to the flow, flux, and difficulty of life, Caputo goes on in the book to explicate what such a radical hermeneutic looks like when practiced in terms of rationality, ethics, and an openness to mystery.

One might ask, *Why is such a long excursus that re-articulates Caputo's radical hermeneutics necessary in an exploration of theopoetics?* I would

---

98. Ibid., 106.

99. Ibid., 111.

100. Ibid.

101. Ibid., 116.

102. Ibid.

103. Caputo, *The Weakness of God*, 299. Fr. *Viens, oui, oui* = Come, yes, yes.

respond by saying, *Caputo's developments are, in my opinion, central and representative of what theopoetic discourse attempts to accomplish, which is placing embodied life central to the discourse. By doing so, he makes room for new ideas, experiences, and life itself.* As such, Caputo's work, finds itself as the centerpiece to my *folded* exploration of theopoetics.

All together Caputo's radical hermeneutics offers a persuasive case that life—phenomenological and linguistic—is interpretive all the way down and calls for a hermeneutic approach.[104] This realization opens up an area for discourse beyond propositions. For all propositions are not only interpretive at the level of reading, but they also entail a multiplicity of interpretive moments: between life and experience, experience and thinking, thinking and writing, writing and reading, reading and speaking, speaking and hearing—all of which are unpredictable and require a movement of repetition that may yield something new in the futural *to come*. It is this openness to novel events, hidden within words, writing, and life more broadly, that leads Caputo to consider theopoetics in his later works.[105]

Caputo's Derridean repetition forward, informed by Kierkegaard among others, occurs not as whimsical chaos, but as a nexus of life, phenomenology, and language. Each momentous moment of life is not entirely disconnected from the past, nor is it determined by it. Derrida's word *différance* helps articulate this as it brings together difference and deferral into one world. The next momentous moment of life, language, or writing occurs in that the future is deferred—it never truly comes— and yet there is a possibility of difference in this never fully arriving to come.[106] Rather than experiencing the arrival, one hears the call of the event, hidden within the word, and is invoked and provoked by speaking it. For example, when one says democracy or justice, what is said or seen in these two words is never the full arrival of the event they invoke but only their arrival in part; therefore, within these words there is a haunting call or solicitation.[107]

It is in this space cleared out from metaphysics and open to a call that Caputo is able to think anew about God. Yet it is not a completely novel *God* but a repetition because he probes "the event that stirs *within*

104. Caputo, *Radical Hermeneutics*, 135.

105. See footnote 10 in my introduction for a brief explanation of *event* as meant by Caputo.

106. Caputo, *Radical Hermeneutics*, 129.

107. Caputo, "Theopoetics as Radical Theology," 132–33.

historical theological reflection."[108] God then, for Caputo, neither exists nor does not exist (onto-theological categories); instead Caputo speaks of God insisting. By this he means that the event of God insists within the word *God*, or alternatively stated, the call insists from the event.[109] It is this call/event that Caputo finds within the Christian tradition. Following Derrida, who would speak of "the impossible" as the new and novel that is made possible by the events within words, Caputo links *the impossible* that is still to come with various aspects of Christianity. For example, he links *the impossible* to the "poetics of the kingdom," which then does not so much draw a straight line to the politics of the current political order but rather frees the political (kingdom) imagination. Thus it is through a poetics that "the kingdom provides a *'politica negativa,'* a critical voice rather like the voice of a prophet against the king, like Amos railing against Jeroboam, calling for the invention of justice."[110]

Here, in the call for justice, Caputo's heady hermeneutical and phenomenological project *touches down* in tangible, practical ways. The motivation—in many ways similar to Alves—is that the current modes of discourse lack the freedom of imagination; the end that has always remained closed and predetermined now requires a radical breaking open to free a newly possible future. Previously, metaphysical assumptions and assertions had put a cap on the spring of life's unforeseen possibilities and dammed the imagination to yield fixed outcomes as determined by rigid constructs. This solidification thereby entrenched the status quo and its systematic and structural oppression that resists the new and takes advantage of the poor and weak in order to benefit the strong and powerful. It is because of his resistance to the metaphysical status quo, its outworking's in an unjust and oppressive system, and a desire to affirm life that Caputo follows Derrida out into the flux beyond law-like structures. It is there beyond the structures, as Derrida writes in his essay "The Force of Law," that one understands the strength of the law is not the structure of the law itself, nor its metaphysical underpinnings. Instead, what gives law force is the call of justice *within* the law, a call that is undeconstructible because it is always coming and never fully arrives.[111]

108. Caputo, *The Insistence of God*, 60.

109. *Insist* as Caputo uses it means "something that does not quite exist but still makes itself felt; something that calls upon us, lures us, solicits us." Caputo, *Hoping Against Hope*, 50.

110. Caputo, *What Would Jesus Deconstruct?*, 87.

111. Derrida, *Acts of Religion*, 233, 243.

Being attentive to such calls from within words is desirable for Caputo because it invokes the possibility of something new. His longing for the event/call is more readily heard in a theo-poetic that opens up rather than a theo-logic that attempts to explain and pin down. Following the call, however, is not necessarily always going to result in positive outcomes, for to guarantee a positive outcome would require a metaphysical certainty that is not available. Rather following the call (even the call within the word *God*) is a risk: the riskiness of life! The outcome is not guaranteed, but such is the pursuit of drawing near to the unknown that is life.

Caputo's theopoetic thinking carves out a small arena that is quite distinct. Caputo explains it this way: "I propose a poetics of the event, a para-logical poetics of the kingdom, a deconstructive or even quasi-phenomenological poetics of the impossible, where an *epoche* is put in place . . . in order to release the structure of the event and to allow ourselves to be overtaken by its life-transforming force."[112] Furthermore, Caputo distinguishes his position from other poetic or romantic thought: "But if poetics is not a 'logic,' neither is it an 'aesthetics.' A poetics is not a theory of art or sensuous feelings; it is not a work of art and it does not mean 'poetry,' even as it does not fall back upon a feeling of dependence ([Friedrich] Schleiermacher). If we were speaking German, I would say poetics concerns *Dichtung*, not *Poesie*, a theory of creative discourse, not of verse."[113] Moreover, Caputo claims, "I am defending a view that poetics is neither an epistemology nor a metaphysics but a certain irregular form of phenomenology."[114] Finally, he contrasts his thinking about the *event* from a return to a spiritual mythology:

> The fundamental tendency of mythic thinking is to turn the insistence of events into beings who do the insisting. . . . In a myth, an event becomes an Uber-being. . . . Theopoetics is not mythopoetics just because it is mytho-poetics demythologized and re-poeticized in a poetics of the event. In theopoetics, everything turns on *rejecting* supernaturalism, that is, the cluster of distinctions between natural and supernatural, transcendence and immanence, reason and faith, human knowledge and divine revelation, and time and eternity.[115]

112. Caputo, *The Weakness of God*, 112.
113. Caputo, *The Insistence of God*, 66.
114. Ibid., 111.
115. Ibid., 97.

Thus, Caputo's radical hermeneutics pushes his theopoetics to the immanent plane, without succumbing to reductionism, determinism, or merely linear logic as his theopoetics provokes the event within confessional theology toward the contingent and the potentially novel in the *to come*, which may or may not arrive—perhaps and perhaps not.

Of note at this point is the work of Peter Rollins who in many ways follows on from Caputo in popularizing a deconstructivist approach to Christianity that is neither theistic nor atheistic, but it rather functions, insists, and provokes the event that lies within Christianity. He is radically iconoclastic in terms of deconstructing idolatry, even idolatry of God.[116] While all of Rollins's books dip into some form of theopoetics, his book *The Orthodox Heretic* presents a series of parables and reflections that lure the reader into a space of deconstruction rather than offer a solid (as solid as deconstruction could be) deconstructive argument.[117] The focus shifts from what is said to how it is said which highlights the experience of the reader. Thus, Rollins enacts a skepticism that authorial intent is all that matters in light of a fuller understanding of a text as "occurring" as a transactional and potentially empty place, a place in which (deconstructive) possibilities reside between the poet/author and the audience/reader. Keefe-Perry highlights a similarity between continental philosophy and theopoetics that Caputo and Rollins utilize: both discourses "offer critiques of 'hollow language,' 'ossified doctrine,' and 'empty doxologies and litanies.'"[118] The possibilities that arise from this nexus of empty spaces are most clearly demonstrated in these two thinkers as they focus on the transformative potential that the reader experiences when encountering a text. This transformation is precisely the point for Rollins, which he emphasizes in his use of transformative art that brings new possibilities out of current circumstances.[119]

### Richard Kearney

From our plunge into the depths beyond metaphysics, we begin our slow ascent out of that whirling current with Kearney. While still phenomenologically and hermeneutically sensitive, his allergy to metaphysics is not

116. Rollins, *The Idolatry of God.*

117. Rollins, *The Orthodox Heretic and Other Impossible Tales.*

118. Keefe-Perry, *Way to Water,* 92.

119. Ibid., 96.

the severe anaphylaxis of Caputo who doubles down to eradicate the contagion at even the most minute whiff of metaphysics.[120] Kearney, alternatively, places language, God, and metaphysics in a state of wager by way of an eschatological gamble. *Is there peanut butter in the cookie or not? You will not know until you try it!* While not yet experiencing anaphylactic shock, Kearney continues the high stakes betting, by splitting the binary of *is* and *is not* with a *may be*. Thus rather than placing a roulette bet on black or red, Kearney bets that *God* will come up the green zero. The stakes are high. As such, Kearney's work is peppered with metaphysical and ontological hints, slants, and echoes. While never completely affirming or denying them, he leaves them in the *might be*, the perhaps. God may be (onto-eschatological)—*and maybe one is not actually allergic to peanut butter*—the wager is not for the faint of heart.[121]

Kearney's project is to "challenge the classic metaphysical tendency to subordinate the possible to the actual as the insufficient to the sufficient" by posing that "it is divinity's very potential-to-be that is the most divine thing about it."[122] Thus Kearney places God in a state of wager: "God will be God at the eschaton"—it is a promise.[123] In framing God as a promise, Kearney posits a third option, the *onto-eschatological*, that attempts to forge a middle ground between ontological and eschatological interpretations of religion.[124]

Kearney makes room for a *third* option by highlighting two downfalls of ontological interpretation and the danger of eschatological interpretation. First, *onto-theology*, which is "the conceptual capture of God as a category of substance,"[125] and second, *mystical ontologism*, which is "the conflation of divine and human consciousness."[126] These both are idolatrous in that the first grasps God and the second deifies humanity. Kearney goes on to state that the *eschatological* interpretation also has its weaknesses—but Kearney argues these weaknesses have precedent within the Bible—in that naming God becomes the ethical pledge of a promise. YHWH as a name-of-invocation means that "Yhwh is revealed

---

120. Kearney, *The God Who May Be*, 5, 7.

121. Ibid., 8.

122. Ibid., 1–2.

123. Ibid., 4.

124. Ibid., 22.

125. Ibid., 24.

126. Ibid., 24–25.

as affected and vulnerable, showing himself henceforth as one who wrestles with himself (Hosea), laments (Jeremiah), regrets (Samuel), seduces and forgives (Psalms)."[127] Yet the name-of-invocation does not have the guarantee of magic utterance. Therefore, eschewing both pitfalls, Kearney attempts a middle way that allows both an ontological and an eschatological approach to interact wherein one can still speak of God without regression to an absolute mysticism that would come from entirely abandoning ontology all the while sidestepping the potential forms of idolatry entailed within ontology and retaining the ethical and communicative interaction between humanity and God offered in an eschatological interpretive framework. As such, Kearney calls his hermeneutic mode of reading God as "may be": "an *onto-eschatological* hermeneutics. Or more simply, a *poetics of the possible*."[128]

Kearney's hermeneutics of religion of a poetic-possible God offers a few insights into how theopoetics might interact with humanity. First, Kearney reinterprets "the 'making mind' as a divine power which empowers, in the sense of enabling and transfiguring, the latent capacities within the human mind" thereby enabling humans to perceive what may be.[129] Second, "divinity is reconceived as that *posse* or *possest* ['possibility-to-be' (*posses esse*), or as Nicholas of Cusa coined the compound term *possest*] which calls and invites us to actualize its proffered possibles by our poetical and ethical actions, contributing to the transfiguration of the world to the extent that we respond to this invitation."[130] Third, rather than Friedrich W. J. Schelling's subordination of the Son and the Spirit, Kearney opts for a more egalitarian direction where "the Father might thus be re-envisaged as the loving-possible which transfigures the Son and the Spirit and is transfigured by them in turn," thereby providing a more egalitarian view of the divine and the cosmos that then has the potential to be more inclusive of, and offer more significance to, human action as integrated through the Son and the Spirit.[131] Insofar as theopoetics participates in making available new possibilities, it enables these three aspects—perception, contribution, and egalitarian community, as they relate to humanity—to come into being.

127. Ibid., 30.
128. Ibid., 37.
129. Ibid., 102.
130. Ibid., 105.
131. Ibid., 106.

## AN ASIDE: A COMPARATIVE ESCHATOLOGICAL ANALOGY

While both Caputo and Kearney prioritize the possible and the futural temporal dimension that theopoetics participates in opening up, they do so in slightly different ways. Perhaps a comparative analogy relating to other major Western theologians of the twentieth century will be helpful for some readers, though certainly not for all, to highlight the difference between Caputo and Kearney on this point of the eschatological *possibles* of humanity's temporal future. Caputo, I think, is analogous to Jürgen Moltmann, while Kearney's analogue is Wolfhart Pannenberg. To be sure, this analogy does not withstand in-depth scrutiny, but for what it is worth I think it is helpful for highlighting the differences. While both Moltmann and Pannenberg wrestle with the futural aspects of theology, they do so differently. Moltmann reframes eschatological hope in terms of promise and fulfillment, which frames his theology in terms of hope.[132] Pannenberg takes Moltmann's usage of promise and adds the proleptic moment of Jesus to project promise back into existence.[133] As such Pannenberg is able to argue from the position of holding an ontological priority of the future,[134] which means "the present is an effect of the future, in contrast to the conventional assumption that past and present are the cause of the future."[135] Such a position then leads Pannenberg to write, "What was new was Jesus' understanding that God's claim on the world is to be viewed exclusively in terms of his coming rule. Thus it is necessary to say that, in a restricted but important sense, God does not yet exist. Since his rule and his being are inseparable, God's being is still in the process of coming to be."[136] Thus the analogy holds insofar as Caputo eschews the existence/non-existence binary in favor of insistence and the *to come* framed as hope beyond hope, which has a certain resonance with Moltmann's focus on promise and hope. While Kearney does not completely eschew language of being but reframes it in an eschatologically

---

132. Moltmann, *Theology of Hope*, 46.

133. Pannenberg, *Systematic Theology*, 3:540.

134. Zehnder, "The Origins and Limitations of Pannenberg's Eschatology," 123.

135. Ibid., 125. Such a position is apparent in *The God Who May Be* when Kearney writes, "The eschaton, like the *angelus novus* blown back against time, comes to us from the future to redeem the past. It is *contre temps*." Kearney, *The God Who May Be*, 82.

136. Pannenberg, "Theology and the Kingdom of God," 7.

futural sense of *may be*, which has a certain echo of Pannenberg's "coming to be."

## Excursus

If one has an evangelical disposition toward faith, belief, and God, then one might wonder whether there is not too much doubt, disbelief, or sheer navel-gazing present in the hermeneutics of those involved in theopoetics. Has God not spoken? Is the Word not clear? Is not the Spirit's role to reveal the things of God (1 Cor 2:10)? Did not the authors of Scripture have specific meanings in mind?

Here I briefly consider two would-be objectors who might argue that theopoetics falls prey to such questioning because it fails to acknowledge the transcendence of God that participates in divine speech (albeit transcendence that resonates with a more classic understanding of the term). The two authors who function as examples of this position since they articulate some of the sentiments behind these possible objections are Klaus Bockmuehl, who links listening to God with a devotional piety that is attentive to a God who speaks, and Nicholas Wolterstorff, who asks, and seeks to answer, some of the challenging philosophical questions that are in proximity to theopoetics. Both of these authors would most likely want to challenge Caputo when he writes a representative theopoetic statement regarding the hermeneutical position of thinking: thinking toward God entails "the mystery which withdraws, which never hands itself over in a form we can trust."[137] Initial analysis might suggest that it is primarily a directional disagreement within humanity's relation to God, and from which side the action begins—the first conception of God speaks and acts toward humans, while the mystery of the other withdraws from the grasps of human. But as I will suggest, I think that the difference goes much deeper and the relation is perhaps more complicated than an initial analysis may lead one to believe.

Bockmuehl offers a devotional approach in *Listening to the God Who Speaks*.[138] The book is a plea for an active listening on the part of the Christian, which is supported by Bockmuehl's strongly held belief that "when people listen, God speaks."[139] The book is primarily di-

---

137. Caputo, *Radical Hermeneutics*, 271.
138. Bockmuehl, *Listening to the God Who Speaks*.
139. Ibid., 8.

rected at those who accept that God has spoken but are doubtful that God still speaks.[140] He recognizes that the continual speaking of God is a large claim and that not all of what arises in quiet listening is from God. Therefore he puts forward the advice to test what one hears against the Bible and the opinions of others who listen to God.[141] Bockmuehl goes on to survey the scriptural witness highlighting that God is a God who continually makes Godself available to his people through speech. And while the Spirit may teach new things, one ought to understand the Spirit together with the other members of the Trinity and interpret reality through a synthesis of the Spirit and Scripture.[142] Bockmuehl concludes by way of warning against both activism and passivism as one listens to God, for activism participates in human pride while passivism does not take seriously enough the task of sanctification.[143] Therefore it is a both/and position of active listening that he implores the reader to adopt.

There are parallels within Bockmuehl's book, and thinking, that resonate with theopoetics, even though he does not associate with the term. His argument for God as one who continually speaks bears some resemblance to a theopoetics that looks forward to the *to come*, the new, and the possible. Both want to engage with God as one who is not confined, completely static, or bound so tightly that all life is restricted. However, the primary difference is that Bockmuehl prioritizes personal listening, prayer, and listening through Scripture (a text already written), whereas theopoetics focuses on enabling God to speak through creative writing, openly reading a multipl*i*city of texts, making space for a new word to be spoken, and thereby assisting a larger society-influencing discourse to be birthed. Much of theopoetics (at least the Derridean strands over against someone like Vahanian, who, in my reading of his work, tends toward an activism) would find common cause in avoiding passivism and activism, at least insofar as it involves hearing from God. For while there is a focus on poiesis as making, or deconstruction as drawing near to the event harbored within a word, there is no guarantee that one will provoke a new word. Therefore, while theopoetics is active, the results are not controlled.

140. Ibid., 9.
141. Ibid., 8.
142. Ibid., 67, 137.
143. Ibid., 141–42.

Wolterstorff's book *Divine Discourse* is a much more charged critique of the positions held by a number of people involved in theopoetics. Wolterstorff begins by locating his topic and clarifying that he is addressing divine speech, not revelation. Within speech he differentiates between *locutionary acts* and *illocutionary acts*: "Locutionary acts are acts of uttering or inscribing words. *Il*-locutionary acts are acts preformed *by way of* locutionary acts, acts such as asking, asserting, commanding, promising, and so forth."[144] Bracketing off the conversation that God speaks by way of sound waves (locutionary acts), Wolterstorff focuses on an argument that God speaks by way of illocutionary acts, speech action that gets things done.[145] In many ways one can understand the position Wolterstorff constructs as being similar to Caputo's focus on the event's agency occurring in the "middle voice," or what "gets itself done" in the saying of a word.[146] Wolterstorff continues by way of analytical, philosophical argumentation in defending this claim that God speaks.[147] Of present relevance, when Wolterstorff arrives at the question of interpretation there are two chapters that are of particular interest: "In defense of authorial-discourse interpretation: *contra* Ricoeur" and "In defense of authorial-discourse interpretation: *contra* Derrida." These chapters are noteworthy because Ricoeur and Derrida are major influences on Kearney and Caputo, respectively. As such, I will take up a discussion of each chapter sequentially.[148]

144. Wolterstorff, *Divine Discourse*, 13.

145. Ibid., 37–42.

146. Caputo, *The Insistence of God*, 31. Caputo's usage of "what is going on" in a word, "is worked out by means of what is called the middle voice in Greek grammar, which is something in between an agent doing things and a recipient receiving them." Caputo, *Hoping against Hope*, 202n16.

147. Wolterstorff's use of analytical philosophy as his discourse is a major difference, both intellectually and stylistically, from other authors considered in this book. Besides occasional exclamation marks at the ends of sentences, which up until that point had not communicated a rhetorical flourish, Wolterstorff's writing lacks a certain *joie de vivre* that is present as a present to the reader in others' writing. That being said, and to his credit, Wolterstorff does adopt a conversational tone in the book so as not to simply drag the reader through endless analytical sequencing.

148. While Wolterstorff's interaction with Ricoeur and Derrida focuses on his critiques—and therefore mine will as well—he does not view all of their thought and development as negative: "Though I won't here emphasize it, very many of the points made by Ricoeur and Derrida are ones that I agree with and also want to make. My response here is not to be understood as unremittingly negative!" Wolterstorff, *Divine Discourse*, 133.

When beginning his critique of Ricoeur, which mainly has to do with hearing God speak when interacting with a text, Wolterstorff highlights the twofold way that God speaks: both "by way of *authoring* the Bible" and "by way of *presenting* someone with a passage."[149] Wolterstorff attempts to keep these aspects connected while Ricoeur allows for more drift to occur between the two. Wolterstorff astutely pinpoints a key difference between his own ontology and Ricoeur's ontology that functions within their differing positions, and this, in my opinion, is precisely that which leads to differing approaches and conclusions. Articulating this difference he writes, "Fundamental to my own ontology of language is the type-token distinction; Ricoeur, by distinguishing between the potentiality and the actuality of particulars, attempts to make do with only particulars in his ontology of language. His crucial move is to think of an event of uttering or inscribing a word as *actualizing* a possibility."[150] Wolterstorff appears to retain a more solid and stable ontology while Ricoeur (and Kearney following suit, as shown above) is more willing to move his ontology into time, which puts it more at risk of the flux of life and leaves it in a state of wager in regard to the future. This temporalizing of the difference between possibility and actuality, which requires *actualizing*, is a reason Ricoeur can create distance between the *authoring* of and the *presenting* of a text—which is important for theopoetics insofar as a new *making* of the text occurs in reading.

Wolterstorff disagrees with what he considers to be Ricoeur's creation of a gap in which "the author is alienated from the interpretive activity" that occurs when one differentiates between "interpreting utterance in the dialogical situation, and interpreting writing in the distanced situation."[151] He considers this to be a failure in Ricoeur's interpretive system because discourse proper, which was central to Ricoeur's understanding of speech action, has disappeared somewhere along the way, as though forgotten.[152] Wolterstorff asks, "How could Ricoeur give central importance to authorial discourse in his philosophy of language, and then, in his theory of interpretation, acknowledge only textual sense interpretation?"[153] However, it is precisely at this point that I think Wolt-

149. Ibid., 131.

150. Ibid., 134.

151. Ibid., 141–48.

152. Ibid., 148–49.

153. Ibid., 149. Wolterstorff clearly summarizes Ricoeur's and his own nuanced positions later on: Ricoeur's argument "was not based, strictly speaking, on a rejection

erstorff's more substantive ontology obscures his clarity of argumentation in that he appears to forget momentarily that Ricoeur has not gotten
rid of the text.[154] Ricoeur maintains the text and adds a second moment
of *actualization* into the interpretive process from the text to the reader;
thus, it becomes at least a two-step process, and the second step assumes
the first step (but it does not negate the first step). To ignore author-to-
text and text-to-reader as a necessarily separate two-part actualization
occurring within time would be to conflate the first step with an author/
text unity, which Wolterstorff nears defending because he concludes that
the sentences and linguistic context interpreted alone are insufficient for
full interpretation. It is my argument, however, that although Ricoeur
moves on from discussing authorial-discourse, he has not removed the
text, and insofar as the text is retained, a discourse with the author is part
of his interpretive schema, just not in the way Wolterstorff desires it to be.
Therefore, it is my opinion that Wolterstorff oversteps in suggesting that
Ricoeur is inconsistent in his usage of authorial-discourse. Instead, I see
Ricoeur moving his articulation of the relation between the author and
the text from an explicit and argued position to an implicit and assumed
aspect of his thought when he is specifically addressing the second step
of the interpretive process.[155] This doubling, two-step process opens up
Ricoeur's interpretive method to more possibilities than are available to a
conflated one-step process.

Having considered Ricoeur, Wolterstorff moves on to consider the
more radical thought of Derrida. Derrida, in the words of Wolterstorff,
"contends that authorial discourse interpretation is untenable because
the very notion of authorial discourse is untenable."[156] This position,

---

of authorial-discourse interpretation, but rather on the claim that to discover the sense
of the text *just is* to discover the content and stance of the authorial discourse. . . . It
was, strictly speaking, an argument against the *autonomy* of authorial-discourse interpretation. And my argument in response was that the content and stance of discourse
cannot, in general, be inferred from the meaning of the sentences *per se* and their
linguistic context." Ibid., 153.

154. My reading of Wolterstorff's type-token distinction leads me to conclude that
it entails a more substance-like existence that transfers through time, rather than potentiality and actuality that have a temporal focus on actualization.

155. One of the ironies in what I am suggesting is that Wolterstorff in an effort to
defend authorial-discourse interpretation ends up missing an implied authorial intent—which he is trying to defend—by Ricoeur that his philosophy of language, which
links the author to the text, remains intact as he moves on to speak about the second
interpretive movement to the reader.

156. Wolterstorff, *Divine Discourse*, 153.

as should be apparent based on the discussion regarding Ricoeur, is an objectionable position for Wolterstorff, but he nonetheless engages it charitably.

After briefly introducing Derrida's thought, Wolterstorff identifies his point of disagreement: "It will turn out that the disagreement between us pivots almost entirely on the status of meaning—or as I shall sometimes also call it, *thought* (using 'thought' to refer to *what is thought* rather than to the thinking)."[157] Again Wolterstorff is astute not only in locating the difference but also in highlighting the point of divergence that causes the differences. Wolterstorff retains "true or false" and "facts—entities in relationship," as understood through an *a priori* metaphysic.[158] As articulated in chapter 1 of this book and the subsection of chapter 3 on Caputo, it is precisely these metaphysical beliefs that are under attack, and, as will be seen in the following section on Keller, need to be updated to more directly align with the real world (i.e., quantum indeterminability). Derrida's post-metaphysical work conversely redefines meaning as being understood *a posteriori*, arising from the *signification*, but not existing anterior to signification.[159] Wolterstorff goes on to discuss Derrida's own position of being implicated in a metaphysic, assessing his project to be an act of resistance to metaphysics.[160] He concludes in a generous way, "Two interpretations of interpretation. I have not argued against the practice of Derrida's alternative. I have only rejected the imperialism of Derrida's rejection of authorial-discourse interpretation—rejected the repression and suppression indigenous to his line of thought, rejected his violence against authors."[161] Similarly, and hopefully generously, I will not here attempt to argue with Wolterstorff's position, or his objections to Derrida, because to do so would be another full book. Instead I submit to you, the reader, that the problems Wolterstorff is wrestling with in Derrida's interpretive theory are some of the underlying problems of theopoetics, which are being investigated and engaged throughout this entire book.

---

157. Ibid., 155.

158. Ibid.

159. Ibid., 159.

160. Ibid., 162–70.

161. Ibid., 169. An alternative position that defends the ethics of reading deconstructively, but would take this work too far afield if pursued, is put forward in Gary A. Phillips's chapter "The Ethics of Reading Deconstructively, or Speaking Face-to-Face: The Samaritan Woman Meets Derrida at the Well," in Malbon and McKnight, *The New Literary Criticism and the New Testament*, 283–325.

The argument of this excursus has been a bit disingenuous insofar as the first part focused on whether or not God has spoken, for many involved in theopoetics do not object to an assertion that God has spoken, or that God continues to speak. Yet, as has been highlighted by Wolterstorff's critiques of Ricoeur and Derrida, the main criticism an evangelical audience may want to levy against theopoetics occurs at a second level of questions: questions of hermeneutics, interpretation, and the mode, manner, and means for understanding and interacting with a speaking God.

Where the tension inevitably resides for me is to what degree Wolterstorff's position is able to account for difference.[162] By prioritizing authorial intent over against the interpretive openness of Ricoeur and Derrida, I wonder whether such a position will not ultimately lead to a totality, or a known universal that will squeeze out difference. Wolterstorff addresses this concern in the chapter "The Illocutionary Stance of the Biblical Narrative," in which he makes room for different genres and differing voices within Scripture. However, I am not yet willing to let go of secondary openness at the interpretive level that authors like Ricoeur and Derrida champion.

Keller poses a question that can function as an example of both the willingness among those engaging in theopoetics to accept that God speaks and the desire to hold interpretive openness. I imagine that this question might be how she would respond to Bockmuehl and Wolterstorff. She asks, "How then could the *question* of God be silenced, except by one final mimesis of His unquestionable voice?"[163] In other words, so long as there is still a question, so long as there are various interpretations of the assertion that God speaks (which will inevitably exist no matter how strong or dogmatically one makes the assertion), how can one fully sidestep the theopoetic project? For the project builds not from a God who does not speak—an absence—but rather it builds (creates a bricolage) from questions—a present absence—such as: Did God speak? Or how do we interpret a God who speaks? Or how do we hear God speaking? Or how do we make room for God's speech? Thus, theopoetics begins from a less certain position but not from a *complete*

162. Wolterstorff's work is not a crushing hegemony or totality because it does include aspects of difference, demonstrated in the chapter "The Many Modes of Discourse." But Wolterstorff's openness to difference is not in the interpretive openness in which much of theopoetics takes place. Wolterstorff, *Divine Discourse*, 37–57.

163. Keller, *Cloud of the Impossible*, 30.

absence. As such, the relationships between the speech, the author, and the interpreter become a bit blurrier, for there has not yet been the "final mimesis of His unquestionable voice." Accepting the blurriness of these relations is a position Keller might call a "mindful unknowing," which I will explore in the next section.[164]

## 3.3—A METAPHYSICAL MOMENT: AN EVENT-IVE RIPPLE

The third stream of this braided river has an entangled and event-ive flow. As the river proceeds toward the ocean, it encounters a congruent tributary in process philosophy and theology. Process thinkers draw heavily on the thought of Whitehead, the wellspring of this creative stream and its focus on the flowing together of all things. While Whitehead's philosophy often makes its way downstream through highly analytical and complex currents, it also entails an elegant and more delicate flow. An example of the latter comes in his description of God as "the poet of the world, [who is] with tender patience leading it by his vision of truth, beauty, and goodness."[165] God's leading, or lure, into the next moment of becoming coincides with the *chaosmos's* (a mix of chaos and cosmos) participation and mutuality in co-creation of the world, a process that is understood as being similar to a poetic/poiesis as *making*.

Of particular interest at this moment where the rippling waters of the streams of theopoetics appear to flow together is the work of Keller, a constructive (as opposed to deconstructive) theologian, who writes at the confluence of the poetic/imaginary/post-DoG/liberation stream and the continental philosophy/phenomenological/hermeneutical stream.[166] Yet what distinguishes her, and those like her (of note is Roland Faber), amidst the generative gurgling of the water is her incorporation of a process (event-based) metaphysic.[167] The waters within this stream of

---

164. Ibid., 22.

165. Whitehead, *Process and Reality*, 346.

166. Keller herself identifies three streams of theopoetics. Keller, "Theopoiesis and the Pluriverse." As named by Keefe-Perry they are: "Eastern church theosis, Hopperian post-Death-of-God scholarship, and the process emphasis on God's multiplicity and infinite becoming." Keefe-Perry, *Way to Water*, 79.

167. Faber, *God as Poet of the World*. This text is not here examined. However, the compilation of essays that came out of a conference interacting with Faber's work is incorporated into this book at various points. Faber and Fackenthal, *Theopoetic Folds*.

thought seem to have unique bonding capabilities that unify without solidity, which enables her to incorporate more broadly Eastern thought, relational ontologies, and scientific inquiry, at the same time as writing at the confluence of theopoiesis and theopoetics—all the while locating herself in the fold between.[168]

## Catherine Keller

Keller's work *Cloud of the Impossible* concludes with a chapter "After: Theopoetics of the Cloud" in which she clearly locates herself in the theopoetic conversation. As articulated in pre-amble-ing, Keller utilizes both theopoiesis and theopoetics. She does so by folding these two approaches together—not identifying them as equivalent or two sides of the same, but rather two sides with unique differences that fold together agreeably. As such, she works poetically both through forming/poiesis and linguistically/deconstructively, all the while relating the entire gamut to the human, the world, and God.[169] Keller's ability to make use of both aspects of theopoetics, while retaining distinction between the two, makes her work unique, complex, and truly interdisciplinary in ways others considered in this book have not been able to accomplish.

Her concluding discussion of theopoetics in *Cloud of the Impossible* does not arrive from nowhere as an add-on to her argument. Rather theopoetics is entangled within her matrix of thought. For example, just as she does not consider the universe to be from nothing, neither does she

---

168. See pre-amble-ing for a discussion of and articulation of the difference between theopoiesis and theopoetics. Others also are working in the nexus of these streams. For example, Luke B. Higgins links poiesis, aesthetics, process, and continental theology, to argue, "If—as I will argue—theopoiesis is uniquely (though not solely) manifest in the emergence and evolutionary elaboration of *life*, this already suggests that life itself—in both its human and non human forms—may be best conceived not as a mechanistic execution of divinely preordained essences or laws but an indeterminate enfolding-unfolding of intensive connections and alliances whose *telos* (to the extent that one can be spoken of) can only really be described in a language of aesthetic valuation." And therefore, this changes our understanding of *telos* and aesthetic derivation, for, "from a creaturely perspective, the initial aim would be experienced not so much as a divine vision 'beamed' directly into our reality from a place of eternal, divine transcendence, but—in a more Deleuzian vein—as a certain capacity to innovatively, virtually 'refract' our own aesthetic, subjective aim *precisely through* the complex folds of its interactions—folds that developed in the first place precisely in and through this process." Higgins, "Consider the Lilies and the Peacocks," 210.

169. Keller, *Cloud of the Impossible*, 306–11.

understand poiesis to be from nothing. She writes, "The poetics by which I have occasionally transcribed logos highlights language as constructive, *poietic*, making something: but never from nothing."[170] She traces creative acts that do not arise from nothing back to pulsating and vibrating potentialities—to the spirit[171] of God hovering over the depths that brings forth multi*pli*cities.[172] Multi*pli*cities then, in turn, are like God in that they are not mere multiples, but a One folded together.[173] What should be becoming apparent is that it is difficult to single out and speak of one part of Keller's thought without considering the entire ecosystem of her intellectual makeup. Therefore, to understand Keller better—where she is writing from and what leads her toward theopoetics—it will be necessary to "be the fish" and swim upstream toward the headwaters.[174]

Upstream we meet a fifteenth-century cardinal Nicholas of Cusa, whose apophatic theology pervades Keller's thought. Following Nicholas, Keller understands apophatism as not mere obfuscating but as a "luminous dark."[175] Therefore, she writes with clarity, but she is also comfortable blurring binaries, folding ideas, and adapting for the future because she believes in openness and the malleability of perspective. Things then do not fall into *are* and *are not*, but rather *coming to be* with varying degrees of clarity. As such, she does not mean apophatism as a simple negation of a positive kataphatic statement, nor as a reason not to ask questions, but the eventual unknowing that results from the world being an open-ended process, where questions may have run as far as possible.[176] She, therefore, classifies her apophatic cloud as being far removed from a willful ignorance but very near a mindful unknowing that one arrives at after *ply*ing the edges of knowing.[177] Perhaps most simply stated, "With Cusa we do not bluntly 'know' anything; we may 'conjecture,' in knowing ignorance."[178]

---

170. Ibid., 309.

171. Keller tends to write spirit with a lowercase "s."

172. Keller, *On the Mystery*, 45–67.

173. Ibid., 49, 64.

174. "Be This Fish" is Keller's chapter title for her chapter on creation, a title she borrows from an analogy used by Bishop Ambrose. Ibid., 45.

175. Ibid., xii.

176. Ibid., xi–xii.

177. Keller, *Cloud of the Impossible*, 22.

178. Keller, "Theopoiesis and the Pluriverse," 188.

Keller applies this Cusian apophatism to theopoetics through two depth-soundings into this "luminous dark": one apophatic, the other deconstructive. Keller explains why the two are distinct: "Deconstruction cannot be identified with negative theology, which remains, after all, theology, indeed a theology indebted to the Neoplatonic One—of which poststructuralism is having *none*. Deconstruction is heir to the legacy of the death of God, the God of ontotheology whose Being *is* that One."[179] Therefore, despite their close resemblance—in that both lead to a type of unknowing—the *a priori* assumptions of apophatism and deconstruction are different. The distinction proposed earlier between theopoiesis and theopoetics would connect negative theology to the former and deconstruction to the latter. However, in Keller's own work, she uses both and speaks of both as a "doubling tension—of a deconstructive apophasis and a prophetic relationalism—[that] forms for the book [*Cloud of the Impossible*] a mobile chiasmus: a co-incident of opposites."[180] Similar to Caputo who favors a method of "crossing wires" and thereby causing a "short circuit" (whether Derrida and Augustine, or Derrida and the Apostle Paul), Keller offers a method of applying the fold as a constructive, chiasmic, collision of opposites.[181] As she makes use of both schemas in her broad theopoetic, interdisciplinary approach—neither conflating the sides of the fold nor severing things from language—she attempts to speak of the real in all its *plies*.

When Keller moves toward an apophatic stance, it is not a nihilistic negation but an unknowing that is open to possibilities, including the possibility of God. She, like Kearney and Caputo, splits the absolutism of theism and atheism (both of which she would say succumb to Whitehead's "fallacy of misplaced concreteness"[182]) with her own process (though not necessarily "progress"): the possibility of coming to be.[183] Through her process metaphysic and apophatic awareness, she links God with the cosmos in a way that unifies but does not identify. This melding, again like Caputo and Kearney, does not move to "a *relativism* of anything goes"; instead, she posits "a *relationalism* of: everything flows."[184]

---

179. Keller, *Cloud of the Impossible*, 8.

180. Ibid., 9.

181. Caputo, *The Weakness of God*, 102; Caputo, *Truth*, 67.

182. Keller, *On the Mystery*, 15.

183. Ibid., 10.

184. Ibid., 14.

Her relationalism, metaphysical process, and ontological entanglement includes God, and therefore God, or theological truth, once entangled, "cannot be captured in propositions no matter how correct. But neither does it [God and theology] happen *without* propositions."[185] Therefore the discourse of theopoetics, like our relationality with all things, calls for a response: participation with language and reality.

Around all aspects of understanding our relationality Keller continues to argue for a cloudy space that does not merely hide but also illuminates in a "brilliant darkness."[186] In this brilliant darkness of the cloud, Keller makes a brilliantly shrouded move that connects language to the physical world through linking nonknowing to nonseparability,[187] via Nicholas's "all in all and each in each."[188] Nicholas of Cusa's articulation of "all in all and each in each," Keller claims, is neither pantheism nor monism, for "God *is* not all things, any more than God *is* any thing."[189] She then can say, with Nicholas, that the universe "resembles God only insofar as it embodies God, everywhere in the universe, equally."[190] The cloudy edges of language's relationship to the material world fold together with the cloudy edges of material reality where each thing participates in "all in all and each in each." The relation, then, between the speaker and listener, the observed and the observer, is a relation that she follows down the fold, right down to the quantum level and all the way up to an entanglement with God.[191] She thereby brings this panentheism into dialogue with quantum entanglement, which is the relation of "bodies all the way down,"[192] arguing this forms the constitutive makeup of the universe.[193] Her quantum-informed, relational, entangled ontology of the

---

185. Ibid., 20.

186. Keller, *Cloud of the Impossible*, 7.

187. Ibid., 89–102.

188. Ibid., 48.

189. Ibid., 94.

190. Ibid., 118.

191. Ibid., 127–67; Keller, *On the Mystery*, 23.

192. Keller, *Cloud of the Impossible*, 122.

193. Faber similarly combines theopoetics and what he calls eco-nature into an eco-theopoetics that highlights the contingency of all things; and he uses poetics for unification without identification: a One-All *with* multiplicity. Faber, "Becoming Intermezzo," 213, 227.

universe strikes a spooky position between Derrida's "hauntology" and a critical realism.[194]

Keller's position between hauntology and critical realism is evident in her response to Albert Einstein's question referencing the indeterminability of quantum fields. Einstein once asked, "Do you really believe the moon is not there if nobody looks?"[195] This question portrays Einstein's disbelief that quantum indeterminability is dependent upon the observer. Keller offers a response: "A moon is there when we are not looking at it. But not as exactly the same moon, not as 'the moon'; not as the self-identical, simply located substance possessed of its properties. Without observers it is a ghost of itself."[196] Likewise, for Keller, God's action and agency are not fully present unless they are actualized by relationality, a position that is well defended by the biblical account of God acting through people. And similarly, when one connects relationality to textuality, the text is not fully *actual* until the reader actualizes the ghost of the text through a participatory relationalism. This relationalism and apophatism then takes her to poetry: "poetry, which plies the edges of language, as metaphors mix, fold, multiply into metonyms for what might occasionally be called an *apophatic theopoetics of relation*."[197]

Theopoetics then, for Keller, is a way into the apophatic future. This is a leading into mystery, not mystification, because "learned ignorance, or mindful unknowing, sanctions not the cancellation of difference but its intensification."[198] It is at the point of the unknown that theopoetics functions best as a lure onward. The cloud of the impossible, which Keller implores the reader to join her in, "does not propose a *return* to the truth of any prior mysticism. Its deep loops of repetition [similar to Caputo via Kierkegaard] unfold now and uncertainly, in an intertextual indeterminacy mindful of its own history of Christian overdetermination."[199] Theopoetics intensifies difference and forces open folds that may potentially be more pleasant if they remained shut—as what is sim*ply* assumed often breaks into multi*pli*city.

194. Keller, *Cloud of the Impossible*, 139.

195. Ibid., 136.

196. Ibid., 141.

197. Ibid., 24.

198. Ibid., 22.

199. Ibid., 18.

With an eye toward multi*pl*icity, what matters, for Keller, is "not what we say *about* God but how we *do* God."[200] Insofar as theopoiesis is *God-making*, the taking place of theopoiesis is the unfolding of God: an active speech.[201] This *doing* God she links with Gregory of Nyssa's *theosis* ("divinization" or becoming God), which is a contraction of theopoiesis.[202] Though one may see this as a positive correlation for theopoetics, Keller argues that it is this ancient connection that has caused process philosophy and process theology to skirt theosis (and theopoiesis) "because it is embedded in classical substance metaphysics, which process means to replace."[203] Yet Keller, a process and relational theologian, still identifies a harmonizing cause in theopoetics, in that both theopoetics and process are against the artificial separation of human identity and divine identity. This is evident, within process thought, in such radical statements as Whitehead's declaration that it is "as true that God creates the world as that the world creates God."[204] With this entangled understanding, Keller claims, "Doing God means acting *not* as separable agents but in differential collectives mindfully enfleshing our planetary entanglement."[205] Yet just when this position of seeming identification is affirmed, the cloudy apophatism that Keller *pl*ies takes hold, and the apophatic *ply* that does the unsaying "will negate this very language of God-making, of divinization, before it congeals—only to say it again, in some moment of the self-implicating inscription of our tiny, humble, and crowded oikos, nerve ending or microorganism, in the unfathomable body of bodies, 'worlds without end.' Amen, almost."[206] The becoming of entanglement is just that, *becoming*, not a *became*.

What Keller argues that theopoetics, or poiesis, can do best is keep the tensions in flux in a way propositional assertions cannot maintain. She writes, "[Like] icon, allegory, paradox, and symbol, metaphor in its time does not escape the threat of reification," for as John Calvin asserted, the heart is "a factory of idols."[207] Thus theopoiesis's focus on *making* keeps

200. Ibid., 306.

201. Ibid.

202. Ibid., 307.

203. Keller, "Theopoiesis and the Pluriverse," 183.

204. Ibid., 183–84.

205. Keller, *Cloud of the Impossible*, 308.

206. Ibid.

207. Ibid., 74.

the metaphor in a state of becoming since "words stretch, crack [and] will not stay still."[208] This then is iconoclastic language that retains a futural wager very near to that of Kearney, and by analogy, to Pannenberg, for "the incarnation remains an experiment, results still indeterminate, in intercarnation."[209]

Finally, one might hear loudest echoes of some currents from the first stream of theopoetics as theopoiesis: imaginative writing that provokes more writing and the *doing* or *making* of God.[210] Yet to group Keller solely with the first stream would be to act too quickly, for she also identifies with *theopoetics* and its deconstructive tendencies that mark "God-talk with its proper im/possibility."[211] Rather than choosing one of the two previous streams, Keller writes, "'Theopoetics as the insistence of a radical theology' [alluding to Caputo] has here quietly been folded together—and never identified—with theopoiesis as the persistence of an ancestral iconoclasm."[212] It is the fold that enables Keller to maintain her own distinct process theopoetic stream that draws upon both of the currents of the other two streams without confusion or mixture. The fold is also her technique for holding together entangled chaosmos, the deconstructive linguistic chasm, the speaker and the spoken, and sub-stantial binaries that fuse into new events, ushering in folds within folds: a multi*pli*city.[213]

## Meanings of "God"

A conversation that occurred at the annual meeting of the American Academy of Religion and Society of Biblical Literature in San Diego, 2014, may help to clarify some of *what/who* is being spoken about/of

208. Ibid.

209. Intercarnation is not a wrong spelling of incarnation; rather, it is a word play on incarnation that highlights the interrelatedness of carnal beings, which God participated with and continues to participate in. Ibid., 315.

210. The first stream should not be understood solely as *theopoiesis* and the second as *theopoetics*. These streams meander through one another, and traits from each of these categories can be found in either stream. Keller's non-identifying fold is precisely between the two categories she sets up, which do not map precisely onto the two streams I have identified.

211. Keller, *Cloud of the Impossible*, 309.

212. Ibid.

213. Ibid.

when each of the above authors uses the term *God*.[214] The conversation was between Caputo, Keller, and John B. Cobb, and it revolved around the question Caputo asked, "Can God die? Or can God be disentangled from the world?" Keller's response was that the word *God* could die. But she then reposed the question more difficultly, asking whether the *referent* to which the word *God* refers could die. To this Cobb answered that the death of God is possible but extremely unlikely.

In order to clarify what he meant, Cobb laid out categories to assist the audience in understanding what was being talked about. He borrowed categories from his professor Richard McKeon at the University of Chicago, who posited that there are a variety of fundamental questions or loci of thought of which McKeon identified three: things, thoughts, and terms. Cobb argued *terms* and *thoughts* can be distinguished, but they are also easily grouped together. The difference then is whether when speaking of God, a person is talking about a *thing* (metaphysics, while also acknowledging God is not a thing) or a *term/thought* (*Geist*/spirit). Relating this to the possibility of the death of God, Cobb argued that DoG theologians were concerned with *Geist* in line with Hegel. Therefore, Cobb claimed they were speaking about *terms* and *thoughts* (*Geist*), which they considered to be the house of being. For those who think in terms of *Geist*, *reality* is understood to be what is conceived of linguistically. Against this, Cobb situated himself and his speech of *God* as speaking of God more so as a *thing*.

If I were to apply this twofold categorization of *things* and *terms/thoughts* to the theopoetic authors primarily dealt with in this book, in a manner following Cobb, it would be as follows. The theopoets of *things* are: Keller, Kearney, Alves, Wilder, Keefe-Perry, and Hopper (perhaps). While the theopoets of *terms/thoughts* are: Vahanian, Caputo, and Hopper (perhaps).[215]

Caputo, however, became perturbed when Cobb categorized him as simply a *Geist* thinker, and labeled him as a DoG theologian along the lines of Thomas Altizer.[216] Caputo adamantly refused the categori-

---

214. Fuller, *The Birth of God and a New JC—Part 2 Keller AAR*.

215. Keller, as shown above, plays in the border region between things and thoughts. However, though she is deconstructively sensitive, she shows her hand: "Words that body forth meaning are not just words. They do not materialize surface without volume, face without deep." This tips her ever so slightly toward a focus on "things" beyond the words. Keller, *Cloud of the Impossible*, 309.

216. One can easily see how Caputo's position might be understood as falling into

zation of being a linguistic idealist or linguistic subjectivist, for like all categorizations, he wants to make them bleed, to *tear*[217] them open and show that ideas influence the real/things/*res*/objective and that these categories do not firmly contain the subject matter.[218] For example, when Caputo claims that God does not *exist* in an onto-theo-logical way but rather *insists* upon our existence, he transgresses categorizations. In doing so he draws near to a process position without establishing or claiming a metaphysic *a priori*, while still saying that ideas/the call of events/language/thoughts/insistence influence/impact/affect existence. One can then see how similar Caputo's position is, *mutatis mutandis*, to a process event metaphysic in which, as an example, prayer actually affects the shaping of the possibilities that God is able to make available as the future. Prayers, in this example, then in their own way are *ideas* affecting *existence*, which process theology and philosophy enable by submitting both ideas and existence to a meta-structure of an event metaphysic of becoming, while Caputo articulates the influence as occurring through a call of an event, and that call's insistence upon existence.

All this to say that there are a variety of meanings, referents, or lack of referent attached to *God* within the theopoetic discourse. Cobb's twofold categorization is helpful insofar as it enables the cloud to shine a little more luminously, revealing two strata that are present. Caputo, in turn, is helpful in blurring the strata back together into one cloud and showing us that neat categorizations are not so easy. In response to both Cobb and Caputo, Keller presents the audience with a dreamy metaphor of a wall within this cloud that becomes a fold. This image is conceptually helpful in stimulating the imagination as it enables the bringing together of distinct categorizations so that they might be reconceived as folds within a multi*pli*city.

---

a *Geist* category because of statements such as, "Where the word fails, the thing itself always slips away" which quoted even slightly out of context or not within a fuller understanding of his perspective appears to reduce the "real" to that which is linguistically communicated. Caputo, *Radical Hermeneutics*, 192.

217. "Tear" can be read with a dual meaning, since the "cut" toward we-know-not-what (the event within the word) will involve the "cries" of those engaged. Caputo, *The Prayers and Tears of Jacques Derrida*, 340.

218. Cobb, however, resists such transgression because he views his own position as one that speaks about the "real," which follows his view that René Descartes and Kant are the most important modern philosophers, whereas Caputo favors Hegel's philosophy.

# Chapter 4

# Aims: Not-Answers

*We are what we eat.*
*We eat what does not exist: dreams.*
*We are the dreams we eat.*
*Dreams are good to eat: food . . .*
*We are transformed by the food we eat.*
*We are transformed by our dreams.*
*We are transformed by what does not exist.*
*"What are we without the help of that which does not exist?"*
*A dream is not a cogent argument.*
*A dream is not a true statement about reality outside.*
*It is not a convincing explanation.*
*It is not a chain of clear and distinct ideas, either.*
*Arguments have no taste,*
*explanations have no odour,*
*clear and distinct ideas don't have colours . . .*
*Images are the presence of the lost object of desire, offered to our senses.*
*They invoke its erotic exuberance: colours, scents, tastes, touches. And the*
*body makes love with the absent and experiences its delight, eschatologi-*
*cally.*
*All lovers know what I mean.*[1]

—RUBEM ALVES

---

1. Alves, *The Poet, the Warrior, the Prophet*, 95.

How does one direct the currents of a river that flows into the wide open? Where should the river flow? Such questions ask, perhaps, too much. For as God asks Job, "Have you entered into the springs of the sea, or walked in the recesses of the deep? Have the gates of death been revealed to you, or have you seen the gates of deep darkness? Have you comprehended the expanse of the earth? Declare, if you know all this."[2] My response is that I certainly cannot declare, but maybe firmly directing a stream is different than whispering where one hopes it might lead, or having felt the currents within the stream suggesting where one might foresee it flowing. As such, it is in this less domineering way that I move on here to discuss some of the ambitions, hopes, and themes of theopoetics, not desiring to close off future possibilities (at least not yet).[3] With an eye toward the possible I will outline eight aims already identified by those engaged in theopoetics—eight, a resurrection number—that the streams and currents within theopoetics flow toward.

## HOLDING TOGETHER

First, theopoetics attempts to hold things together. But this *holding together* is not like nails tearing through flesh and wood to pin down and bind, but more so an embrace or a coming alongside of a crying woman in a garden. This mannerism has already been witnessed previously—language (Vahanian), *différance* (Caputo via Derrida), apophatic folds (Keller)—through the use of poetic writing. Poetics more readily accepts apparent contradictions, dichotomies, and paradoxes than does propositional argumentation.[4] This implementation of poetics, however, raises a second question of how philosophy and poetics are to relate.[5] For what do we do when people walk through walls and enter rooms that remain

---

2. Job 38:16–18 NRSV.

3. Harrity et al. communicate a similar sentiment: "One does not come to theopoetics to have their questions *answered*, one comes to have them *opened*. Theopoetics thrives within the discomforts of begging truth to be revealed, not basking in the sun of the known." Harrity et al., "The Theopoetics of Literature: An Aesthetic Statement."

4. Sobolev, *The Split World of Gerard Manley Hopkins*, 302.

5. Blake Huggins notes this tension between philosophy and poetry goes back at least as far as Plato's discussion of it in "Republic, which means it is even more "primordial" than Tertullian's tension between Athens and Greece. Huggins, "Introduction," 1–8.

locked? While various ways are hinted at above, two further examples will suffice here.

What does it mean to *touch* and *see* when it comes to writing, or to *place* your hand here, and look at the *wound* there when reading? In his essay "Reality, Eternality, and Colors: Rimbaud, Whitehead, Stevens," Michael Halewood argues that a move to theopoetics adds a qualitative element to thought, which has a tendency to be reduced to quantitative assessment of concepts, and therefore theopoetics is actually more truly empirical than common, merely logical approaches.[6] He argues, by way of analogy, that in the same way "vowels are the breath of language" the rigidity of concepts needs the breath of poiesis, and vice versa, in order to be real. This reality is a symbiosis, for "the friction and fricative-ness of consonants requires the openness and liquidity of vowels as much as the vowels require consonants simply to be able to end, become finite and grant sense."[7] He moves on to conclude, via Whitehead, that philosophy and poetry cannot remain distinct, but neither should they be identified. For philosophy would lose its critical effectiveness and poetry would lose its "ability to utilize language as a way of challenging the boundaries of our thought"; therefore, rather than being identical to each other, one should think, "philosophy is *akin* to poetry."[8] Thus he proposes a cooperative relationship between philosophy and poetry, where the hand touches and the eye sees, and the ear hears and the wound is felt in all of its fullness.

Who sees first? Or maybe that is the wrong question, and it would be better to ask, is it the eye, or the ear, or the hand that encounters reality initially? Hollis Phelps takes the relationship between poetry and philosophy further in his daring essay, "(Theo)poetic Naming and the Advent of Truth: The Function of Poetics in the Philosophy of Alain Badiou." Alain Badiou is a French philosopher whose intellectual project is an attempt to "construct a contemporary systematic philosophy, the parameters of which revolve around the articulation of a mathematical, and hence rational and deductive, ontology and non-objective or generic theory of truth and the subject."[9] Phelps argues, however, that Badiou's

---

6. Halewood, "Reality, Eternality, and Colors," 15, 18.

7. Ibid., 16–17.

8. Ibid., 27–28.

9. Phelps, "(Theo)poetic Naming and the Advent of Truths," 30.

mathematical ontology is predicated on a prior poetic truth.[10] He argues that Badiou constructs his mathematical ontology as a predicate to events, and "the event occurs at the limits of *dianoia*, or discursive thought, meaning that the latter cannot grasp the events."[11] Thus the event must be named in order to enter discursive thought, which means a poetic supplement is added to the event.[12] Once discursive, the event then is made available to the construction of truths, whether mathematical or otherwise. Combined with a Whiteheadian understanding of God as the one who makes possible new events that are then to be named,[13] Phelps concludes, "It is the poetic element, necessary for the production of all truths, that seems to imply a theopoetics, even if Badiou would not recognize it as such."[14] Thus Phelps, by way of Badiou, predicates philosophy on a (theo)poetic. So perhaps it is not the eye and its divisions that must welcome life first—"Blessed are those who have not seen."[15]

While there is not a consensus regarding how to think philosophy and poetry together or how to bring together dualities, those championing theopoetics are arguing with a renewed vigor that these various aspects of human thought need to be brought together.[16] These two examples, articulated by Halewood and Phelps, offer potential ways forward for thinking about how a theopoetic—specifically the poetic, discursive, and artistic elements, that move beyond logical, mathematical, and representational abstractions—might relate back to philosophy once a stream of thought has led to theopoetics, which is investigating these relations. Perhaps the emptiness of the tomb—as a *present absence*—offers both more and less clarity regarding the relation between discourses than many might desire.

10. Ibid., 43.

11. Ibid., 42.

12. Ibid., 43.

13. Ibid., 44.

14. Ibid., 45.

15. John 20:29 NRSV.

16. A further option that may yield fruitful returns, though not one fully worked out specifically in terms of theopoetics, would be the application of Ian McGilchrist's two ways of knowing. Where the rational, narrow, logical, linear, and focused way of knowing is the emissary that must serve the master, which is a broad, metaphorical, intuitive, and imaginative way of knowing. McGilchrist, *The Master and His Emissary.* I am pleased that Loren Wilkinson has chosen to begin to work this option out in the foreword to this book.

## INTENDING EXUBERANCE

Second, theopoetics plays with and intends exuberance—an energy not dissimilar to a frantic footrace against a friend. Wilder draws together poetic imagination and celebration when he writes, "Imagination is a necessary component of all profound knowing and celebration; all remembering, realizing, and anticipating; all faith, hope, and love."[17] Knowledge and celebration come together in life and imagination, and theopoetics attempts to blend them in a *joie de vivre*. Caputo develops a similar sentiment toward play in his theopoetics as well as adding a meditative element, writing: "Derrida's deconstructive work issues in grammatological exuberance which celebrates diversity, repetition, alteration. Heidegger's deconstructive work issues in a meditative stillness, which could not be more alert to the play in which all things are swept, but it is stunned by the power of this sweep and culminates in a deep sense of the play in which mortals play out their allotted time."[18] Thus Caputo's radical hermeneutics attempts to blend ecstasy with contemplative stillness and wonder, both of which can be understood as exuberance for life. Finally on this note of exuberance, I offer to you an extended quote from Vahanian that shows something of this wonder, play, and excess that is pumping forth from physicality—an energy like that of a disciple who is not quite sure where the footrace will end—which is the joy of theopoetics:

> But listen again, lend an ear to scientists, and grant them that nothing is in the outer language what was not in the inner language of the self, in the physio-bio-neurological tissues of sound and noises muted in that inner language of the self that, confined as it were to "that which has been said," does not yet speak. But then no sooner does it speak than lips are raised into words, onomatopoeia into metaphor, flesh into spirit or the world of how and what to that of a world that is all that is the case.
>
> Bursting, language overflows, it exceeds every limit of that which has been said and weaves a fabric of words telling not only what is said but also what is being said and done that possibly could point to that which henceforth cannot not be said—in that order, and which hence, in the light of biblical vision, time

---

17. Wilder, *Theopoetic*, 2.
18. Caputo, *Radical Hermeneutics*, 206.

is construed as present and sole instance of that which, time and again, lasts once and for all. Here and now.[19]

## Making Space

Third, theopoetics offers space/*Gelassenheit*. Caputo articulates the direction of this current, "Radical hermeneutics does not leave us in the lurch but rather gives us room to stretch our intellectual limbs."[20] The wide-open space at the end of a river *becomes* a wide-open tomb. I may venture in and stay a while; there is even a spot to rest my head, but my way is not sealed. There is no stone that retains me, rather the tomb, the closed word, the caging word, becomes a room. This *room* is then effective in affecting all other aspects of life: from thought, to language, to ethics. It remains uncertain whether this tomb-room is good or bad, for it cannot guarantee either a peaceful sleep or sweet dreams; too much remains undetermined for such conclusions. *For if the tomb is open and empty, are the ghosts free to go where they will?* While the creation of space is a theme in theopoetics—since it privileges the future and makes room for imagining possibilities—there is not a consensus regarding precisely how or in what way this space should be understood. The tomb is empty, that much we know, but how and why this room is given remains as elusive as trying to grasp empty space itself. However, while a consensus is lacking, the prevalence of this current that flows toward an open door deserves a more extended exploration. What follows is my own attempt to swim about within this open sea, to walk about this open room, and to survey the wondrous space of the open tomb.

Most simply, *Gelassenheit* means to let something be or to offer another thing space. *Letting be* or *making space* was popularized by Heidegger's term *Gelassenheit*, but he did not originate the idea; Kearney shows Heidegger borrowed *Gelassenheit* from the Catholic mystic Meister Eckhart.[21] Caputo deepens Heidegger's explanation of what he means by the word: "'*Gelassenheit*' refers not only to thinking but also to that which grants thinking, which admits thinking into its sphere, which lets things (*Dinge*) be, and, finally, as the other side of the horizon, which

---

19. Vahanian, *Theopoetics of the Word*, 60.
20. Caputo, *Radical Hermeneutics*, 213.
21. Kearney, *The God Who May Be*, 93.

lets the horizon of objects be."[22] Caputo contrasts this phenomenologically derived, ontological understanding of the open sea of *Gelassenheit* to other terms that mean similar things: "In metaphysics this goes under the name of 'contingency,' but in religion it is called grace. Our lives are a series of ongoing run-ins with the aleatory, where 'free' and 'conscious intentions' run up against the anonymous play in things. We are asked to stay in play with this play, to play along with its open-endedness, to keep open the space of the gift."[23] What we do with this gift is of course up to us, but the givenness of the gift remains quite startling and unasked for.

Whatever one calls it, *Gelassenheit* is an intrinsically ethical idea, for it only comes to be when ap*plie*d. Highlighting this active nature, Caputo writes,

> We want to think *Gelassenheit* towards others, the sense of respect or reverence the other commands, which arises from the fact that we know that here we are dealing with deep waters. Other persons are places in the flux where deep waters whirl about in a particularly bewildering way, where the woods are particularly dark and deep, where the cloud formations are mysterious, perplexing, inviting, even frightening.[24]

Thus *Gelassenheit*, when applied, offers the other space, and in return, it makes room in oneself for the "deep waters" of the other, which is the making possible of an ethical relation with the other.

Yet, while *Gelassenheit* contains an ethics of respect, it is by no means an impotent idea/disposition, for "*Gelassenheit* is a certain transgression of the ruling power plays which dominate our world."[25] There are no borders that contain the sea, and through one's respect for others—by letting the other be—forms of hierarchy are put into a state of play, and existing edifices that are built upon oppressing or subjugating the other are toppled because an independence, rather than mere subjugation, is gifted to the other. In many ways it is a disruptive ethic, which Caputo highlights as distinguishing his ethics of *Gelassenheit* from metaphysically grounded ethics and also from eschatological ethics (such as Heidegger's—by which he means ethics deriving from the truth or meaning

---

22. Caputo, *Radical Hermeneutics*, 101.
23. Caputo, *The Insistence of God*, 119.
24. Caputo, *Radical Hermeneutics*, 267.
25. Ibid., 205.

of being[26] and entail a nostalgia for a lost past and a waiting for an eschatological reversal).[27] Caputo's ethics is one of "coping with the flux" in our
present world: "We do not act on unshakable grounds but in order to do
what we can, taking what action seems wise, and not without misgivings
(Kierkegaard called it 'fear and trembling'). We act, but we understand
that we are not situated safely above the flux, that we have not secured any
transcendental high ground, that we do not have a view of the whole."[28]
In many ways this sounds like a situational ethics of the sea and it is, but
it retains a level of anxiety and nervousness that not all Christian ethical
schemas contain.[29] The uncertain openness of theopoetics, which entails
an ethic of *making space*, therefore, is not naïvely docile but potentially
quite radical in its practical outworking insofar as it frees the other by
offering space.

Kearney, in turn, concludes *The God Who May Be* with an intentional focus on space, and making space in a subsection entitled "Godplay."
Drawing heavily on Heidegger's assessment of the room at this point,
Kearney explores the idea that "the most simple things may participate
in the ontological 'play of the world' once transfigured by the poet or
the artist."[30] Thus theopoetics opens space where the "thing things" and
the "world worlds."[31] Where the space allows things to be (*Gelassenheit*),
and one takes on a Heideggerian "releasement toward things."[32] Kearney
supports his argument by rooting such a disposition—and the proposal
that there is indeed a *room*—in the very life of God (instead of Caputo's
root in the flux of life). At this point Kearney brings in *kenosis* (Phil 2:7)
as letting go, whereby "God thus empowers our human powerlessness by
giving away his power, by possibilising us and our good actions—so that

---

26. Ibid., 238.

27. Ibid., 242, 248.

28. Ibid., 239.

29. For example, John Stackhouse's argument in *Making the Best of It* is for a form
of situational ethics. But he argues that one in the end acts in confidence, a position
Caputo cannot affirm. However, even Stackhouse admits to "trembling" when affirming Bonhoeffer's actions: "I myself have come to the awful conclusion that Bonhoeffer
was right to participate in the plot against Hitler, and I submit it here with trembling."
Stackhouse, *Making the Best of It*, 286.

30. Kearney, *The God Who May Be*, 106.

31. Ibid. NB: He also draws upon the thought of the poet Gerard Manley Hopkins
at various points, but this aspect of Kearney's thought is not further considered here.

32. Heidegger, *Discourse on Thinking*, 54.

we may supplement and co-accomplish creation."[33] Through the divine life Kearney reframes Heideggarian ontological releasement/*Gelassenheit* into an onto-eschatological framework that opens up space for what *may be* in a futural sense.

Kearney further develops this futural openness by not only arguing that space is created in the actions of God toward humanity but also within Godself through the *perichoresis* of the Godhead, which creates *room* for God. It is helpful to quote Kearney at length on this point:

> God-play was known as *perichoresis* in Greek and as *circumin-cessio* in Latin. Meaning literally "dance (*choros*) around (*peri*)," it referred to a circular movement where Father, Son, and Spirit gave place to each other in a gesture of reciprocal disposition rather than fusing into a single substance. The Latin spells this out intriguingly by punning on the dual phonetic connotations of *circum-in-sessio* (from *sedo*, to sit or assume a position) and *circum-in-cession* (from *cedo*, to cede, give way or disposition). So what emerges is an image of the three distinct persons moving *toward* each other in a gesture of immanence and *away from* each other in a gesture of transcendence. At once belonging and distance. Moving in and out of position. An interplay of loving and letting go.[34]

Kearney's postmodern Trinity—prioritizing dynamism rather than stability—highlights the space creation that occurs within the Godhead. This focal point of making space is an aspect of relationship that some articulations of the Trinity do not maintain when they too heavily focus on the action toward the other through mutual indwelling or interpenetration of the three persons.[35] Such conceptions focus on the presences being *in* the other persons of the Trinity, and in so doing, they reduce the sense of *letting be* that also occurs between the persons.

Kearney's articulation of the Trinity offers theopoetics, from the center of Godself, the space to say and not say; to write and leave blank space; to articulate and wait for a response within the discourse itself.

33. Kearney, *The God Who May Be*, 108.

34. Ibid., 109.

35. It is precisely on this point that Jens Zimmermann critiques Kearney. For according to Zimmermann, adding *chora* (an empty center) to the Trinity's *perichoresis* adds a different "substance" to the Trinity than that of its persons. This fits with Zimmermann's larger argument that the answers reside in a return to an "orthodox" substance metaphysic of the creeds, rather than the postmodern alternatives. Zimmermann, *Incarnational Humanism*, 240–42.

Rather than attempting to write it all—which is analogous to a conception of the Trinity that merely focuses on the indwelling without including the letting be—Kearney offers each individual *room* to come toward a God who may be, through onto-eschatological readings of texts. Writing without space cannot be read and speaking without space cannot be heard.

Keller, because of her willingness to engage metaphysics and ontology, redefines the premises of making space to be radically non-hierarchal by way of basing it on a relational and entangled ontology.[36] She challenges the premise of one giving space to the other to the extent that such a premise may put the first in a position of power over the second, or paradoxically the first may subjugate the second as a means to make space for that second. An entanglement such as Keller's brings us to an open tomb, where death and life are not each other's antithesis as in Heidegger's being-toward-death—whereby an over and against logic must function to create a priority of one over the other—but death and life are entangled with/in each other. From this entangled premise Keller argues that to love one's neighbor is to love God, and vice versa, as both are enfolded in one another. Therefore, there is no priority of loving God in order to love my neighbor, or loving my neighbor in order to love God, for both relegate one aspect to a means for the other.[37] The entanglement of God in a relational ontology, wherein the created order can impinge upon God, enables her to make such radical statements of mutuality. Keller writes,

> If it is a divine choice not to control, a choice to *let be*, then perhaps we need to understand this choice as the very meaning of what we call "God": the letting-be at the heart of the universe. Or starting up a universe, as Genesis 1 poetically captures it. And this divine freedom to create depends upon the responsive freedom of the creatures, the lapping and overlapping influences flowing upon the face of the deep.[38]

36. Others who make use of a process metaphysic, however, retain a more clearly defined place for space/*khora*. For example, Higgins places space as central. He writes, "I spoke earlier of the 'chaotic nexus' at the 'base' of the universe—a structure of utterly open-ended connectedness identified with the idea of empty space. It turns out that the entirely living nexus is *also* said to occur primarily in a region of empty space—this time, the empty space opened up in the 'interstices' of the body and the brain." Higgins, "Consider the Lilies and the Peacocks," 206–7.

37. Keller, *Cloud of the Impossible*, 291.

38. Keller, *On the Mystery*, 89.

Thus the *letting be* and the action toward (the *cedo* and the *sedo*) are nearly identified, but not quite.[39]

Nevertheless, Keller nears forming a universal (unifying the *sedo* and the *cedo*, or God and the world), which she does not shy away from because the universal is always ineffable and shrouded by the cloud of unknowing. Furthermore, following Alain Badiou, Keller argues that it is repression in the name of the dominant particular—not the universal—that leads to the death camps.[40] For Keller, then, it is not God as the signifier for the universal that is the problem because by definition such a universal is apophatically open, but it is an idolatrous understanding of God as particular entity that then fails to make space for the other. She refers to an insight by Kearney that it is only the demons (Mark 1:25) that claim to *know* Jesus in a categorical-identity type of way, without appropriate apophatic openness.[41] Therefore, because of her apophatic framing of a universal as an open multi*pli*city with folds within folds, Keller in many ways is able to sidestep the need to incorporate *Gelassenheit*. She arrives at the benefits of making space without some of the particular hang-ups that may come from Heidegger's thought. Her mix of apophatism and relational ontology create an open rationality, theopoetics, and ethics that enforce neither a dominant totality nor a space without relational responsibility.

## (Re)Locating Transcendence

Fourth, as noted in chapter 1, the relocation of transcendence is an ongoing task of modern and postmodern theologies; therefore, the retention of transcendence remains a hope that is part of the open meal of fish on a beachside served up by theopoetics. Moreover, as theopoetics participates in *Gelassenheit*, and other ways of incorporating space for living and eating a meal, it is involved in *flattening out* the Western metaphysical hierarchies (i.e., higher and lower, master and slave, rich and poor), which means transcendence also needs to be creatively reframed from *above and below* to an alternative conception. The work of Levinas

---

39. You, the reader, should remember at this point that no matter how closely Keller might identify things the ever-present apophatic protection of the cloud retains a distinction, therefore God is not merely identified with the created order, nor would life and death become synonymous.

40. Keller, *Cloud of the Impossible*, 299.

41. Ibid., 293.

is where many writers of theopoetics turn for assistance in translating transcendence from *above* into a relational transcendence *between*.

Levinas develops his relational metaphysic in *Totality and Infinity* in which he states, "This book then does present itself as a defense of subjectivity, but it will apprehend the subjectivity not at the level of its purely egoist protestation against totality, nor in its anguish before death [Heidegger], but as founded in the idea of infinity."[42] This infinity is not imparted from a preconception but arises within the relation. Moreover, for Levinas, "The idea of infinity is the mode of being, the *infinition*, of infinity. Infinity does not first exist, and *then* reveal itself. Its infinition is produced as revelation, as a positing of its idea in *me*."[43] Those borrowing from Levinas, then, move transcendence from an anagogical vertical space to a horizontal *between* within immanence, which Levinas communicates as occurring in meeting "face to face."[44] For it is in the face of the other, according to Levinas, that this infinity is produced—an open meal of fish *becomes* divine encounter through eating face to face.

Caputo builds on Levinas when articulating the mystery and transcendence needed in his thought. He writes:

> I take my point of departure from the human face, the surface of the face, the face as sur-face over the flux. . . . Flickering in the twilight of presence/absence, the face is a mysterious (Heidegger) and undecidable (Derrida) form. We catch a glimpse momentarily, *augenblicklich*, in the blink of an eye, of a light in the eye of the other, which leaves us wondering, puzzled, provoked. It is the "face" as the most conspicuous point of access, the outermost surface of our body, which opens the way to the recess, the "ground" of the soul, its most hidden chambers.[45]

In this section Caputo moves beyond Levinas by dwelling on the very particulars of the face that reveal a depth (echoes of Tillich, from whom Caputo considers his own work to descend)[46] within the immanent and perceptible.

Kearney also picks up on Levinas's relation to the other beyond totality (history, reason, representation, horizon, power—ontology), and

---

42. Levinas, *Totality and Infinity*, 26.

43. Ibid.

44. Ibid., 79–81.

45. Caputo, *Radical Hermeneutics*, 272.

46. Caputo, *The Insistence of God*, 87.

moves it toward a futural relation—one maybe would say a banquet that
is to come of which fish on a fire is a foretaste.[47] He begins by aligning with
Levinas that ethics are found "in the absolute surplus of the other with
respect to the same who desires him."[48] This surplus is the ineffable and
irreducible, which calls for an ethic that protects it. Kearney helpfully explains how this is translation of transcendence from *beyond* as lack, to an
infinity *between* as anticipation: "The good *beyond* finds itself inscribed
*between* one another. Desire here again reveals itself not as deficiency
but as positivity. Not as *manqué-à-être* but as a grace and gratuity, gift
and surplus. Less as insufficiency than as a bursting forth of the 'more' in
the 'less.'"[49] Kearney is here reframing desire in an eschatological framework that moves desire from an ontological lack of presence needing to
be filled (a hole to be filled—Calvinist total depravity or psychoanalytic
*manqué*/lack), to a desire of the infinite that is beyond and still to come
in each and every instant of life (an anticipation of a gift—a meal always
being offered). Thus Kearney draws very near to Caputo in not searching
for a return to a state before *loss*, but anticipates the *to come*, which moves
toward the ethics of the child: to birth and a future. For the child is a
stranger, "who is me as a *stranger to myself*."[50]

Alternatively stated, Alves spins together this development that
moves from the ethics of history/narrative toward futural otherness
(transcendence) found in the child:

> Did it really happen?
> Had they been really beautiful, somewhere in the past? Did they
> see the magic mirror of their dreams a face as it had actually
> been, once?
> Once?
> When was that?
> "Once upon a time"—thus begin all children's stories.
> My daughter, when she was a small girl, always wanted to know
> if the story I was about to tell had actually taken place. And I
> found it difficult to explain.[51]

---

47. Kearney, *The God Who May Be*, 62.

48. Levinas, *Totality and Infinity*, 97.

49. Kearney, *The God Who May Be*, 64.

50. Ibid., 67. At this point one might consider the story of Abraham and the possibility of eternal existence and salvation through lineage and the hope of a child, rather
than otherworldly existence.

51. Alves, *The Poet, the Warrior, the Prophet*, 41.

Relation here moves from a one-to-one correlation (history equates to ethics) where the *same* is repeated from the past into the future, to a relation as *birth* where something novel is made possible in each new moment of the story—where what was not possible before the gift of a meal becomes possible. This move toward the future brings forth an ethics because the surplus created in the *child* is not reducible to the sum of its parts. Therefore, by way of incorporating time as worthy of ethical reflection transcendence/surplus/infinity finds its place within immanence, both between those relating (face to face) and before the future that is to come (the child).

The ethical move toward the child and the future is part of retaining transcendence in a late twentieth-century context. One can see it as a response to the modern world, in that as metaphysical hierarchies are flattened, one no longer acts out of the great chain of being, nor even in one's hierarchy of priority before death, but in the asymmetrical relation between oneself and the infinity of the other.[52] "Thus in contrast to Heidegger's being-toward-death," according to Kearney, a poetics implores the reader toward the child, and "Levinas (like [Hannah] Arendt) promotes the idea of beginning-again-through-the-birth-of-another. Ethics of natality rather than as mortality."[53] It is a move of ethics from death (or being-toward-death) to life. Alves dreamily writes this development together in the following way:

> Life comes from the dead man of the sea:
> baptism, diving into the depths of the dark waters . . .
> And then, one is a child again . . .
> And the village is never the same again . . .[54]

To sum up, this reframing of transcendence into the immanent world opens possibility for an ethics of surplus within the immanent. In relation to theopoetics, this surplus is also respected in art and writing by allowing the actual paint on the canvas, words on the page, and fish on a fire active participation in making meaning, not merely as a means to

---

52. The relation is asymmetrical because "the face of the Other at each moment destroys and overflows the plastic image it leaves me." Or framed in terms of the "event": the effects of the event exceed the cause of the event. The surplus always exceeds expectation, rather than a lack that needs to be filled—a hilarious generosity of grace/gift, not a merely sufficient amount. Levinas, *Totality and Infinity*, 51.

53. Kearney, *The God Who May Be*, 68.

54. Alves, *The Poet, the Warrior, the Prophet*, 57.

communicate or transmit an abstract thought or idea.[55] The hermeneutical and interpretive openness also adds space for a surplus of meaning by opening a space for transcendence between two *faces*—canvas and the viewer, words and the reader, etc. This inclusion of the material is in stark contrast to an approach to a poetic and the world that defers to a spiritualized, anagogical, vertical, near platonic participation in a metaphysical sense, in which the meaning resides *a priori* to engagement with the art or the words—either in the mind of the author, or an abstracted *real*. Reconciliation came into being as the fish were fried, the meal was eaten, and words were spoken.

## EMBODIMENT

Fifth, embodiment pervades theopoetics. As theopoetics flows away from the heritage of abstraction in platonic metaphysics, it pulses toward the heart of human embodiedness. Our hearts burn within us as we walk a long dusty road together, and our humanity flourishes as we invite the stranger to stay with us because it is nearly evening. Regarding the contrast between abstraction and the body Kearney writes, "In short, unlike Platonic love, this incarnational love of the Bible *does* involve all the senses—sound, odor, touch, sight, taste—but unlike the old pagan rites of sexual fusion and sacrifice, it resists the phallic illusion of totality, finality, or fullness."[56] Theopoetic writing, insofar as it guided by this current, attempts to write *to* the body *from* embodiedness, and therefore, according to Kearney, "a powerful religious poetics can sing the unsayable and intimate the unnameable by means of an innovative and insubordinate language, a language resistant to both allegorist abstraction and metaphysical dualism."[57] As Alves might articulate, this way of doing language and writing attempts both to speak from the body and to eat the words with the body, for eyes open when the bread is broken and food distributed. The words are food that feed, and as Alves states,

---

55. For an interesting parallel regarding ritual communication through music and transmission communication through referential language, which correlates to valuing poetic and metaphorical language see: McGilchrist, *The Master and His Emissary*, 123.

56. Kearney, *The God Who May Be*, 59.

57. Ibid., 57.

> [The] mouth is the place of eating long before it is the place of
> speaking. Eating precedes speaking. Our original Word is a twin
> sister of food. When Ludwig Feuerbach, a professional of words,
> said that "we are what we eat" (man ist was man isst) he pointed
> to the place where Word and flesh make love. "I eat, therefore I
> am." Eating comes before speaking. And speaking, throughout
> our whole lives, is a form of eating.[58]

Words and flesh are forever interconnected within the body, which
means that the body must remain central to theopoetics. How else are
we to share bread with our companions and have our eyes opened if we
cannot go to them?

Various authors of theopoetics incorporate an embodied aspect into
their writing in different ways. For example, Keefe-Perry concludes a section that situates his writing in the following way: "I write as a hopeful,
clumsy, white, married, bisexual, Quaker man and father. I write fully-
fleshed."[59] He thereby abjures any notion of writing from an objective or
disembodied perspective. Differently, Keller incorporates herself by addressing the reader more directly and situating her physical, emotional,
and temporal location when writing. For example, early in her book
*Cloud of the Impossible* she writes, "Such sanctuary practice may be a gift
of theology's currently acute vulnerability. And in the personal context in
which I first wrote this sentence (my mother Jane gradually dying in the
next room), I am mindful of the proximity of hospitality to *hospice*."[60]
Then later in the book she writes, "Anthropocentric individualism has accompanied the denial of mourning. Its displacement does not guarantee
a mindful alternative. But it makes it possible. My sister was mourning
the deaths of two dogs when our mother died. These griefs do not can-
cel each other. She lived them through a vitally entwined process."[61] In
writing this way Keller brings her life, her personality, and herself more
fully into the work by subtly letting the reader know about the death of
her mother through scattered asides. These are just two representative
examples of the various ways authors of theopoetics journey down the
dusty road together with the reader by incorporating aspects of their embodiedness into their writing.

---

58. Alves, *The Poet, the Warrior, the Prophet*, 76.

59. Keefe-Perry, *Way to Water*, 5.

60. Keller, *Cloud of the Impossible*, 27–28.

61. Ibid., 235.

## INDIVIDUALS

Sixth, the aspects of making space, retaining transcendence, and affirming embodiment—all present within the currents of theopoetics—stream together toward vigorous protection of the individual. The meeting and transforming of single persons takes on many modes, some by way of imaginative visions and others through a bright light on the road. One may be tempted to dismiss such a heightened defense of individuality as merely a postmodern obsession with the particular. But to do so would be to miss the nuanced position articulated between extremes that tend toward all or nothing. Affirming individuality is an attempt to carve out a position between totality and nihilistic obliteration. Kearney makes this point precisely by relating it to God and how God has communicated with humanity. He writes:

> God speaks not through monuments of power and pomp but in stories and acts of love and justice, the giving to the least of creatures, the caring for orphans, widows, and strangers; stories and acts which bear testimony—as transfiguring gestures do—to that God of little things that comes and goes, like the thin small voice, like the burning bush, like the voice crying out in the wilderness, like the word made flesh, like the wind that blows where it wills.[62]

Thus it is a God-like mode of speech and writing that validates the person, the story, the poetic, and all particulars, which does not obliterate any of them through a crushing act of powerful speech.

Keller in turn communicates the protection of individuals in terms of power and relation, for without care both power and relation could be manipulated into persecution. She writes, "We are in each other's power. But power does not mean dominance. Power is manifest concretely in the flow of influence, the flow of me into your experience, of you into mine, by which we consciously and unconsciously affect each other."[63] Theopoetics attempts to communicate with this same kind of relationalism and delicacy by broadening interpretation and enabling the participation of each individual author and reader—thereby offering power to both. Keller goes on in a discussion regarding power to say: "A 'power made perfect in weakness' is neither omnipotence nor impotence. . . . This is a power

---

62. Kearney, *The God Who May Be*, 51.
63. Keller, *On the Mystery*, 80.

that does not overpower but empowers."[64] By not utilizing overpowering or domineering propositions that one must accept or refuse on the threat of death, even while they might temporarily blind, theopoetics is a way of communicating in an interdependent way between the author and the reader, acknowledging the active participation of both in constructing the meaning, and in constructing/creating God as communicated. In this way theopoetics attempts to participate in the intellectual protection of the individual reader, by guiding, illuminating, and showing, rather than forcing or coercing intellectual compliance.

## RESPONSIBILITY

Seventh, the flow of theopoetics in its relation to individual protection, and the potential of consequential turbulence, also implores those engaged to take seriously responsibility for human agency. As words become more human and humans become more aware of their involvement in words, the stories that are told to one another become the responsibility of those who hear. Caputo asserts that the task of converting "poetics into reality falls squarely on our shoulders."[65] Caputo explains the interrelated ethical responsibility this way: "The same ancient 'thinking' [poetics] which Heidegger celebrates is inextricably interwoven with ancient politics, ethics, economics, and the rest. There is no clean break between primordial *ethos* and ethics, between primordial *polis* and politics."[66] As such, Caputo aligns with Alves's larger liberation push toward ethical, non-oppressive speech and writing. The entailed awareness of the agency of writing makes theopoetics more than aesthetics as it transforms it into ethics, politics, and economics all at once. With awareness that thought is action and action is thought, theopoetics as discourse is already active and is provoking more action. Because of these interrelations humans become responsible not only for what they *do* but also what they *think*, since the distinction between the two has become blurred.

Kearney and Keller also highlight the responsibility of action to which those participating in theopoetics are called, which parallels in

---

64. Ibid., 85.

65. Caputo, *What Would Jesus Deconstruct?*, 134.

66. Caputo, *Radical Hermeneutics*, 251. Caputo and Keller further explore the interconnectedness between theology, *theopoetics* and *theopolitics* in Caputo and Keller, "Theopoetic/Theopolitic."

ethics developments in writing and interpretation—a much more active engagement by the individual. For Kearney, again, his position follows from his understanding of God, a God who *may be*, which means that since "God is *posse* (the possibility of being) rather than *esse* (the actuality of being as fait accompli), the promise remains powerless until and unless we *respond* to it."[67] Keller's line of thought goes even further and broadens the im*pli*cations via her entangled relationalism. Keller quotes William Connolly's hope that people will "act in concerted ways to defeat neo-liberalism, to curtail climate change, to reduce inequality, and to instil a vibrant pluralist spirituality into democratic machines that have lost too much of their vitality."[68] Keller's im*pli*cation is that humans are responsible for these things draws on Nicholas of Cusa's *possest* (fusing *posse* and *est*),[69] which means *God can make possible*, but "if posse ipsum unfolds or contracts in actualization, it is we ourselves who *do* it. Who *ply*, who layer, fold, and do it. We might not. But we *can*."[70] It is this call to ply the possibilities made available in theopoetics that requires humans to respond, for us to actualize or *make God* real in the existence of the world. For all these authors, the responsibility of humans is now more pertinent than ever since humanity must respond to the "impending ecological catastrophe."[71] Insofar as theopoetics participates in announcing a new life, it also is calling for a responsible enacting of that new creation.

## NEW LIFE

Eighth, theopoetics resist idolatry and ossification, by favoring new life. In the various ways theopoetics is connected to deconstruction, or speaking/writing near apophatic limits, theopoetics resists permanence in favor of play. This play can occur in many ways, often employing parables and poetic metaphors in order to resist problematic propositions. Keller articulates it this way:

> Parables are shibboleth-resistant micro-narratives. They thwart theological abstractions from the start. "Nothing could be more unauthoritative than the parables of Jesus," according to one

67. Kearney, *The God Who May Be*, 4.
68. Keller, *Cloud of the Impossible*, 311.
69. Ibid., 110.
70. Ibid., 112.
71. Ibid., 120.

leading scholar. "Their whole purpose is to enable the listener to discover something . . ." The word *parable* first means "to set or throw to the side," as in making a comparison, an analogy, a metaphoric link between a concrete story and a more elusive meaning: truth not told straight but slant.[72]

Insofar as God *lives*, propositional language will continue to fail to correlate directly to God, or fully correspond to humanity that lives anew in the resurrection life. Keller goes on to draw upon Dominic Crossan, stating, "Parables give God room."[73] Thus theopoetics can be understood as humanity's way of returning the favor and extending *Gelassenheit* to God. For in theopoetics, there is intentional space for the interpreter, the new, the novel, and the possible—all spaces in which God can play and resist the ossification of the grave.

72. Keller, *On the Mystery*, 137.

73. Ibid., 155.

# Chapter 5

# Delineating a Bricolage Pitch: Game-Play of God-Talk in Our Time

*Thus lives the warrior, born out of visions of beauty:*
*with one eye he sees darkness and pain,*
*but with the other he sees light and joy.*[1]

—RUBEM ALVES

THEOPOETICS PLAYS IN AN arena with relativism, but to play on this pitch does not mean that all forms of theopoetics are nihilistically relativistic; their relativism does not necessarily lead to no meaning or a complete lack of guided discourse or direction.[2] As argued above, by the majority of the authors considered, one does not need absolutism to avoid absolute relativism. The game of theopoetics plays by different rules, clues, and suggestions, while at the same time eschewing suggestions, clues,

---

1. Alves, *The Poet, the Warrior, the Prophet*, 120.

2. In fact, for Caputo there is a "certain religion that resides *within* the very cosmic nihilism [Jean-François Lyotard] described," a kind of "nihilism of grace," that includes and will not disavow "hope, the reality of the material world, and (an oddly religionless) religion." Caputo, *Hoping Against Hope*, 18–19. Here again Caputo wounds a binary—this time *purpose is good and nihilism is bad*—and as it bleeds out the pitch is stained with our own blood and the neat and tidy answers and bandages that once hid our trauma darken into a deep maroon and no longer suffice.

and rules.[3] For just when the pitch begins to feel flat, it yaws, pitches, and rolls like a sloop on the sea, and the angle of play must alter to match the new pitch of the pitch. As the play adapts, the player may find that this is the oddest of games: the pitcher is pitching; the pitch shot may land on the green; the tents all may be pitched while the choir sings the perfect pitch that is drowned by the roar of the crowd as it reaches a deafening pitch. But all is not certain—the climber's rope may snag on the final pitch, or the pitch may turn just as sticky as pitch, and as hope fades, all play might come to be nothing more than hide-and-go-seek played in the pitch black. The game moves, not only the players; the pitch is alive, like a text ever-unfolding, and the players play because life de(e)pends o(i)n it. So while the pitch of theopoetics does not lack a goal(s)—as shown in the previous chapter, there are numerous aims that the currents of theopoetics flow toward—it also has numerous difficulties, limits, and notes of caution provided by the players.

I imagine the theopoetics pitch to be much like a game played by a child on a rainy day where every piece of furniture *becomes* an obstacle and an opportunity. The task remains moving around the *living room*, and rules are amassed and broken by equally creative strokes of the imagination. However, instead of a singular goal it has an incredibly complex, and multidimensional goal(s)—as complicated as life itself. Within the game obstacles and limits are set up and torn down; rules form and dissolve; challenges are overcome by those entangled within the web of the game—those pitching the pitch of the pitch. So, in the same way theopoetics eschews a clear definition, so too it abjures a perfectly clear and delineated goal(s), rule(s), and limit(s). In my imagination, the pitch is populated with multiple goal posts and obstacles and is demarcated by various boundaries that are variously arranged by the bricolage nature of the game; therefore, the play of the game is both defined and undefined all at once.

The goal(s) of theopoetics is/(are) neither narrow nor wide, neither obvious nor obscure, neither easy to score in nor is it impossible to do so; therefore, there is no reason to rule out the possibility of a particularly creative theopoetic shot finding its way into the net (though no system exists for tallying points). The goal(s), obstacles, limits, rules, and notes of caution may overlap, apparently contradict each other, or appear to be located on seemingly different parts of the field, and of course, all of these

3. For more on eschewing rules that pin down see the introduction.

are liable to move unexpectedly. My limited objective in this chapter is to locate and articulate where those who are already playing theopoetics, in this potentially relativistic arena, have named and located various aspects of the theopoetics pitch. I am not attempting to systematize or arrange the goal posts into a clearly defined net at one end of the field, nor am I going to kick a ball in its direction. Rather, I will identify some of the limits, obstacles, and notes of caution already present so that future players of theopoetics may join the game already knowing some of the important aspects of the pitch.

## Pragmatism: The Child Lacking Imagination

The first potential limit is a pragmatic objection. One might be inclined to argue: "We cannot function without taming the wildness of the play, without *imposing* normality, without certain measure of stilling the flux."[4] *The game is too obscure, too convoluted, and too flexible! Therefore, let's set up some rules.* Derrida, says Caputo, would not object to this felt human need, but he would want to remind us that there is a "coefficient of uncertainty attached to all such fiction/truths" and that "we must not mistake our need for these 'truths' as something which justifies or grounds normality in principle."[5] Or, more succinctly stated: simply because something *is* (our desire for stability) does not mean it *ought* to be (or actually corresponds to real life). As such, pragmatisms will inevitably be a part of the game as a human desire, but if one defaults too quickly to the status quo, never challenging the hegemony of pragmatic rules governing the game there will never be any opportunity for a novel breakthrough. Or in the case of theopoetics, such a pragmatic clamping-down may inhibit the space made available for the life of God within God-talk.

## Feuerbach: The Fiery Brook

An inverse of a pragmatic restriction (we need stability, therefore it is) is the limit of *no limit* to anthropocentric projection (we see stability, therefore we must have projected it): the Feuerbachian limit. If theopoetics is nothing more than an exercise of corporate (or personal) projection, then, for a number of those involved in theopoetics, theopoetics is a dead

4. Caputo, *Radical Hermeneutics*, 145.
5. Ibid.

end. For the fiery brook will burn up the thirst quenching waters of the river. Feuerbach's critique of Christian religion is clearly stated in *The Essence of Christianity*. For Feuerbach, religion is essentially human feeling corporately projected as the predicate of God (God is ____), and then humanity makes itself an object to this projected image.[6] The solution then, for Feuerbach, is for humanity to switch the subject and predicate of the propositional statements and realize its own projection.[7] For example if *God is Love*, then *Love is God*, so as mature humanity, we should focus on following the way of love.[8]

Theopoets offer a number of responses to the charge that their works fall prey to the Feuerbachian, or a subsequent and similar, critique of religion. Keller, for one, responds by using embodied language to move away from propositions and *is* statements. Keller addresses Feuerbach's critique by highlighting that there are only two *is* statements about God in the Bible, two propositions: "God is spirit," which Jesus speaks to the woman by the well (John 4:24), and "God is love" (1 John 4:8).[9] Instead of using or creating more reversible statements like these, Keller uses active language that is not as grammatically open to inversion. For example, rather than simply stating, "God is infinite," Keller carefully draws upon biblical illustrations that imply active involvement to articulate God's infinity as bringing forward possibility. She writes, "Yet the infinity, as we have meditated upon it earlier, within the doctrinal symbol of creation, may be called the *depth* of God, the creative womb of all that is."[10] Thus

---

6. Feuerbach, *The Essence of Christianity*, 25.

7. Commenting on what Whitehead called "substantialism," which is rooted in Christian and Greek philosophy, Faber states, "Whitehead claimed that this mode [substantialism] of constructing reality is deeply inscribed in languages that use a subject-predicate form such that it divides our perception of reality itself into independent existents without any inner relation but only with derivative forms of participation." Therefore, as a process theopoetics recreates language to fit an alternative metaphysic the *Feuerbachian Flip* loses some of it persuasiveness, insofar as the subject-predicate language construction—grounded in a substance interpretation of reality, which Feuerbach flips—is reconceived of in terms of relationality between all things, even words within sentences. Faber, "Becoming Intermezzo," 215.

8. Alternatively stated, "The essential standpoint of religion is the practical or subjective. The end of religion is the welfare, the salvation, the ultimate felicity of man; the relation of man to God is nothing else than his relation to his own spiritual good; God is the realised salvation of the soul, or the unlimited power of effecting the salvation, the bliss of man." Feuerbach, *The Essence of Christianity*, 153.

9. Keller, *On the Mystery*, 32.

10. Ibid., 99.

she draws on metaphors as a way of mitigating Feuerbach's reversal of the subject and predicate.

Caputo responds to Feuerbach in his own way, by contrasting projectiles and projections. Projectiles, like the event and the call, come over us and come at us, while the projections come from within us.[11] Caputo situates the event in the *to come* (that which we do not see coming). As such, it is not a mere projection—from humanity's present into the future or onto the heavens. Caputo writes, "God calls; we respond. This is at the far remove from projection. It is willing to be exposed to the worst."[12] Moreover, Caputo's theopoetics wrestles with the difficulty of life and does not guarantee any answers or any certainty that is part of Feuerbach's optimism, and in this way he undercuts projection as wish fulfillment. For Caputo, insofar as the unconditioned and uncontainable event is invoked, provoked, and solicited in the call from within the name *God*, the outcome is unpredictable—a perhaps. Caputo wields a double-edged sword of *perhaps* against Feuerbach: he slices away any certainty that religion is nothing but projection, but at the same time, he exposes himself to the more uncertain, second edge that all God-talk still may be all projection, but we cannot quite be sure. This guarded position does not burn away and fall into the Feuerbachian brook because it is not built like a castle on pilings of tinder easily set aflame. The unpredictability of Caputo's schema of the event *to come* is only *perhaps* capable of preventing his version of theopoetics from being simply cast away into the fiery brook as merely a Feuerbachian projection—but perhaps *perhaps* is enough to continue playing the game.

Kearney *maybe* makes the broadest claim that theopoetics does not succumb to Feuerbach. Precisely because theopoetics looks for *more* than what is said, it does not follow the reductionism inherent in Feuerbach's critique of religion. Kearney develops this *more* through argumentation in reference to God's being: "The ontological proposition *esse est Deus* and the theological proposition *Deus est est* mutually deconstruct each other. . . . There's more to God than being. Granted. But to pass *beyond* being you have to pass *through* it. Without the flesh of the word, there is no birth."[13] Thus Kearney's articulation of the "God who may be" goes

11. Caputo, *The Insistence of God*, 27–28.

12. Ibid., 29.

13. Kearney, *The God Who May Be*, 36. *Being is God* and *God is Being* are both potentially reductionist in that the statements assume *Being* is what *exists*, but do not entertain the possibility of that which is *beyond Being* or *otherwise than Being*. As

through *being*—thereby including all that *being* entails—to say something more by way of possibility, rather than allowing God to be reduced
to—and identified as—merely *being*. For such a reduction and identification of God and *being* would allow for Feuerbach's subject and predicate
reversal because the inversion functions on an assumption of the equality
of terms.

Though unique in responding to Feuerbach's critique of religion
each of these authors respect it as a limit but reject, for various reasons,
that theopoetics is nothing more than anthropological projection, as
such they bridge, transgress, and redirect the play of theopoetics away
from and beyond the Feuerbachian fiery brook.


## Oppression . . . Liberation? No Bullies Allowed

A rule that Keller forcefully asserts is that the theopoetics game must not
be played if it becomes a way for language to cover over oppression. She
writes that theopoetics fails if it cedes "strength to the certainties of the
religious right and the atheist left, now, when the eco-democratic alternative so needs spiritual planetary enlivening."[14] Therefore, while Keller
hears the harmonious resonances between theopoetics with its openness
to the future and an ongoing eco-democratic planetary entanglement,
she contends that should the use of theopoetics risk the protection of
the world or humans by way of its *softer* discourse it must be dismissed.
Moreover, Keller argues, "If theopoetics *does* weaken the capacity of process theologians to make confident arguments in debates, in teaching,
preaching and pastoral care, then I would not indulge in it."[15] The manifestation of theopoetics that Keller's rule protects against mainly exists
in a possible iteration of the game where theopoetics *replaces* theology;
therefore, Keller goes on, "But inasmuch as theopoetics serves in the Derridean sense as a 'supplement,' not a suppression or a supersession, then,
far from undermining theology, it enhances its future likelihood."[16] This

---

such, Kearney moves to the excess of *more* such that *more* is inclusive of *Being* but not
reduced to only *Being*; articulated as a move in the God-talk game as *through* Being.
The subject and predicate—God and Being—are thereby asymmetrically related and
not equated, which problematizes a simplistic inversion of the terms.

14. Keller, "Theopoiesis and the Pluriverse," 180.

15. Ibid.

16. Ibid. Huggins articulates Derrida's supplement this way, "What Jacques Derrida
has called the logic of supplementarity, i.e., to the practice of writing as an instance of

enhancement that theopoetics as a supplement offers is a beneficial gift because theopoetics "works to uncork the effervescence of language, the force of metaphor, icon, and story" and therefore adds weight to protecting the environment and the oppressed.[17] Keller's forceful rule-like assertion actually becomes more like a word of caution because she does not think that those traits that her assertion protects against are necessarily an integral aspect of theopoetics.

Regarding Keller's concerns, Keefe-Perry highlights an interesting tension in her argumentation. Keller argues that a process metaphysic assists in protecting oppressed people even though this opens her up to the charge of idol worship because her process metaphysic inherently is an abstraction and idol worship (abstractions) is potentially dehumanizing insofar as it prioritizes the idol over the wellbeing of humans.[18] Keefe-Perry synthesizes the tension this way: "she is willing to accept the charge of idol worship in turn for being able to articulate challenge to oppression."[19] Thus in order to choose life over an abstraction or reduction, Keller disavows life by positing an abstraction as the guard to protect life. In doing so she distinguishes herself clearly from alternative forms of theopoetics, such as Caputo's, that risk everything (accepting an uncertain outcome) in order to draw near to life. Keefe-Perry at this point hedges that Keller's use of abstraction may in fact be necessary in order to affirm life, but he openly wonders if speech that forcefully protects human life necessarily needs to involve abstraction or be conducted as "point and counterpoint."[20] There is, therefore, no consensus regarding how to resist oppression, in terms of which mode of speech or which abstractions are appropriate, but only a general agreement that oppression must be opposed as the game of theopoetics continues to be played.

---

doubling through the (re)production of that which both adds to and presents itself—within and against the present—as a substitute to an 'origin' which is itself supplementary. Supplementary writing, writing as supplement, writing the supplement, minds this gap or split between discourses or disciplines—and within subjectivity itself—by functioning as a cut or caesura at the joints of experience, gathering itself together where sinew meets bone and vice versa. As a supplemental practice, then, theopoetics functions within not without theology." Huggins, "Introduction," 3.

17. Keller, "Theopoiesis and the Pluriverse," 180.

18. Keefe-Perry, *Way to Water*, 82; Keller, "Theopoiesis and the Pluriverse," 187.

19. Keefe-Perry, *Way to Water*, 82.

20. Ibid., 83n41.

## AESTHETICS: SNAPDRAGONS OVER SNARES

A sideline of the pitch is the assertion that theopoetics must not just be the *prettying up* of rational (logos centric) theology or hiding pernicious traps below benevolent guises. This sideline is often flirted with, moved beyond, and blurred as the game progresses. However, the purpose of asserting the line—even if one is not immediately ruled out-of-bounds when transgressing the line—is to caution against hiding predetermined conclusions by merely constructing a façade that depicts open possibilities. For if theopoetics is just theopoetry, it is nothing more than idolatry—that which contains, pins down, and abstracts—in a pretty exterior, or a distraction from the Christian life and action. At a minimum, as Wilder articulates, the aesthetic and the theology must work together: "It is not here implied that imagery and ritual are more crucial than Christian love and action. But significant action needs to be oriented and empowered by a true vision and meaningful celebration."[21] Theopoetics, therefore, must be active in developing thought and participating in the Christian life, and should not be merely a secondary aesthetic veneer or a primary idolatrous beauty. This suggestion may at some level obfuscate clarity in terms of relating beauty to ideas as they are both utilized within theopoetics. For it may at first appear that this sideline requires the placement of aesthetic aspects of theopoetics—which open up possibilities—as the primary action and clarity as secondary. Yet the second assertion is that aesthetics cannot be primary, for then it would become idolatrous in demoting Christian life and action to a secondary tier. Such is the problem of ranking binary categorizations.

I propose that the way through the snapdragons and snares is by way of symbiosis. Theopoetics, inclusive of its beautiful aspects, is relevant and viable in the twenty-first century so long as the aesthetic aspects are advanced in concert with life, action, and thought. At the same time, I affirm with Wilder that an integration of a poetic imagination and theology will remain confusing if "it [aesthetics and the imagination] is set over against the will and looked on as merely decorative. Or [if] it is set over against the will and looked on as frivolous. [Or if it is] set over revelation itself and looked on as idolatrous."[22] However, I do not think

21. Wilder, *Theopoetic*, 3.

22. Ibid., 41. Wilder here is in part taking aim at neoorthodoxy, within a larger tradition, regarding the priority of the will: "Neoorthodoxy, for its part, also disparaged the imagination in favor of the will, the eye of vision in favor of the ear of obedience. It

that these potential weaknesses preclude theopoetics, only those types of theopoetics that are primarily understood as a separate thing, a complete schism and detachment, from traditional categories, histories, ideas, and lived experiences. The way forward in the play of the game, then, is for theopoetics to engage theos and poiesis, aesthetics and ideas, life and action, the will and the imagination, in some form of symbiosis. For if the game of theopoetics fails to deeply entangle itself into the very doing and forming of our God-talk, it is likely to fall into one or more of the snares Wilder identifies.

## Language: Losing Ourselves within the Game

Part of the theopoetics project and its generative God-talk, especially in Wilder's articulation of it, is a renewing of language and the imagination. This renewal is a tentative word of caution for those who desire to join the game because, as Wilder is aware, renewing language can be costly and traumatic. He writes, "Before we join the chorus of those who repeat that the renewal of Christianity is a matter of the renewal of its language we should recognize how difficult this is."[23] When dramatic change occurs an experience of loss often accompanies the transition. For some people this loss will mean that the project is not worth pursuing and the game is not worth the risk. Others may later reach the same conclusion—that quitting the game is the best option—when they realize that "all such recipes and programmed strategies [of renewal] fall short of accounting for the full mystery of language where deep calls to deep."[24] Such discouragement ought to be expected because *falling short* means that the renewal of language, by way of theopoetics, is an ongoing and never concluded project. The pitch has an eerie resonance to the childhood song "This is the song that never ends."

Taking on a project that will never conclude, and playing a game that is never complete, and singing a song that never ends, will always be accompanied by feelings of frustration and loss as the game, the pitch, and the players all continue to change, and the self attached to each of those will be lost as the next iteration of the game comes to be. I offer,

---

seemed to be thought that God or the Word could address us without taking account of how language works." Ibid., 54.

23. Wilder, *Theopoetic*, 5.

24. Ibid., 6.

those who wish to play, this warning about the costliness of the game being played, the loss of language and the self that is attached to that language, and the necessary resolve required of each player who chooses to enter the arena.[25]

## MYSTERY: KNOWNS, KNOWN UNKNOWNS, UNKNOWN KNOWNS, AND UNKNOWN UNKNOWNS

While probing the depths and skirting the edges of this dynamic pitch, mystery will likely be encountered, but theopoetics must not turn mystery into mystification. While theopoetics releases a firm grasp of clear, definable concepts, in favor of metaphor and a poetic imagination, this can turn into mystification that obscures clarity too readily. A play that retreats to obfuscation too quickly might easily turn the pitch into pitch black and can be used to cover over a plethora of wrongs. Keller is aware of this potential problem, writing, "Often what is called 'mystery' (as in 'Don't ask questions, it is a holy mystery') is mere mystification, used to camouflage the power drives of those who don't want to be questioned."[26] For example, mystification often occurs when negative theology is invoked as *God's ways are higher than our ways*, which prevents wrestling with the questions at hand and can defend potentially problematic understandings of God that are sometimes physically and psychologically harmful.

Alternatively, one can find the same trend of rapid mystification on the deconstruction side of theopoetics even though it was precisely mystification that Derrida wanted to avoid. Caputo explains, "Now 'mystery'[27] is one of those words which Derrida always ducks. He does not want the disseminative play to become a negative theology."[28] Derrida's contempt toward negative theology can be understood in that it covers

---

25. Here I am reminded of Heidegger's use of *anxiety*, not as a negative but in which "lies the possibility of a distinctive disclosure, since anxiety individualizes." Heidegger, *Being and Time*, 191. Similarly, I do not view the loss of language as a negative, it may be difficult and traumatic but there may be opportunities for new, life-giving words to arise out of the death of the old language.

26. Keller, *On the Mystery*, xi.

27. Here I understand "mystery" to be closer to what I am calling "mystification," because there seems to be a lot of mystery left in Derrida's thought, alongside a strong theme of refusing easy answers.

28. Caputo, *Radical Hermeneutics*, 201.

over and obscures the tensions in which deconstruction plays and where deconstruction finds *différance* that makes room for the event (not to mention that classically negative theology relates to a metaphysic Derrida disavows). Keller, respecting Derrida's position, attempts to set the limits on mystery so that it avoids mystification: "What a constructive apophaticism in its solicitation of its past must avoid is both foreclosure by knowledge or by the knowledge of not-knowing: the fixing of the mystical 'no trespassing' signs on the boundary of the unknowable."[29] Like edges of a metaphor, where it is *pli*able, mystery must also acknowledge its blurry edges and tension, which means that *mystery* should not be asserted too readily or dogmatically as a means to quick answers that would inevitably vacate vast sections of the playable field.[30]

## The Middle: The Dynamic Cushion on the Couch

A blurry mysticism also assists theopoetics in finding the life-giving space between the limits of rampant relativism and stringent absolutism. As the players play, moving around the living room, there often develops a favorite location to inhabit, the most life-giving and useful location— for me this often was the middle of the couch. From there I could leap to the coffee table, or scurry to the edge of the couch, or throw a pillow to make an *island* on the floor. As I imagine the game of theopoetics, there are various *middles*, but Kearney perhaps most clearly articulates the benefits and life-giving area that is the middle of the couch. He does so by developing the limits of his *metaxology* (middle way, middle-logic). For Kearney this game must be played between two extremes—two ends of the couch—that he links to two views of God:

---

29. Keller, *Cloud of the Impossible*, 61.

30. I think of my time playing on the soaking wet soccer pitches in northern England. The game would commence as normal, even when a corner was completely covered in water and had a seemingly endless mud supply hidden below its depths. So long as there was not an adult presently protecting the corner and telling us not to go there (analogous to holding up a big "mystery do not enter" sign), the play on the field was often drawn to this corner. The one nearing *the abyss* had the advantage since they always had one more option of play available than did the others who remained on *terra firma* a greater distance from the gargantuan mud puddle. It is not that those plays always worked out, or that those of us who risked becoming a soaking wet mess for the rest of the day never were condemned to such a fate, but when those plays were made from the *deep* end of the pitch we all intuited that the play had been worth the risk. The mystery of the puddle did not limit us—it *deepened* our play.

Namely: (a) the hyper-ascendant deity of mystical or negative theology; and (b) the consigning of the sacred to the domain of abyssal abjection. In the first instance, God can take the form of a divinity so far beyond-being (Levinas, Marion, and at times even Derrida) that no hermeneutics of interpreting, imagining, symbolizing, or narrativizing is really acceptable. . . . In the second instance, the divine slips *beneath* the grid of symbolic and imaginary expression, back into some primordial zero-point of unnameability which is variously called "monstrous" (Campbell, Zizek), "sublime" ([Jean-François] Lyotard), "abject" ([Julia] Kristeva), or "an-khorite" (Caputo).[31]

Therefore, even within all of theopoetics' discussion of *more*, *excess*, and *potential*, Kearney asserts a limit. He critiques Marion's saturated phenomenon of *hyper-excess*, which always is ineffable and cannot be understood. If God is only *hyper-excess*, "this mystical experience takes the form of a certain 'stupor' or 'terror' which its very 'incomprehensibility' imposes on us."[32] At such an extreme, Kearney inquires as to whether it blurs and completely obfuscates the distinction between good and evil, through a completely other mystical encounter.[33]

The other limit is where God would slip below the conscious (i.e., Hopper), and humanity would have no power over its thoughts and symbols; they simply would manifest in different forms throughout time. At either limit of ineffable or unconscious there seems to be no way to tell up from down, or right from wrong. Kearney concludes, "In sum, the danger of God without being is that of an alterity so 'other' that it becomes impossible to distinguish it from monstrosity—mystical or sublime."[34] Kearney's *metaxology* is aiming between these extremes, attempting by way of an *onto-eschatological* understanding of God to retain right and wrong and alterity by placing being and ethics in a state of wager—both *may be*. He sets two limits beyond which he considers one condemned to absolute relativism, points at which the couch ceases to offer a life-giving bounce.

31. Kearney, *The God Who May Be*, 7. Perhaps my own preference for middles and the middle of the couch is a result of being a middle child. Situated between two brothers it was necessary that I always kept one eye open to plan my next move.

32. Ibid., 32.

33. Ibid., 33.

34. Ibid., 34.

## HUMAN: FULLY HUMAN

Such extremes of alterity push theopoetics back to a middle, from which comes the assertion that theopoetics must remain human, all too human. This requirement for the game is defended in a variety of ways, but integral to the God-talk game of theopoetics is that *human* must be said in the most full, robust articulation possible, not succumbing to reductionisms. Caputo links being human to an anti-reductionism in play: "We can teach the computer to work but not to play (it can only play rule-governed games)."[35] Thus theopoetics ought to remain "without why," engaging in play for the sake of play, it must have a *joie de vivre* and a resilience to affirm life against oppression.[36] Wilder adds that human theopoetics must be both open to and wary of culture, as well as being open to inwardness but not at the expense of human outwardness because only together do these create a dynamic sense of reality.[37] Wilder is aware that finding this balanced humanness in theopoetics is always a tension: Theopoetics "must assert the rights of the imagination against abstraction, rationalism, and stereotype. But the enemy is also on the other side: the cult of the imagination for itself alone; vision, phantasy, ecstasy for their own sakes; creativity, spontaneity on their own without roots, without tradition, without discipline."[38] Thus the *human* entangled within the game is not so much a stake in the ground as it is a wonderful tightrope wire that somehow is imaginatively incorporated into the game and the use and defense of *human* by the players, it seems to me, is integral for scoring a goal.

## MASKS: WHICH PER-SONA PLAYS?

Finally, another note of caution is given. The caution is that when we vivify masks with poiesis—animating the face of the surface, hinting at a depth behind by sounding through the mask—the activity always entails danger. Who we play when we play can change the odds of the game leading to life or leading to death. In the same way that the mask of the oracle of Delphi in the sanctuary of Apollo was vivified through a poiesis of the

---

35. Caputo, *Radical Hermeneutics*, 227.

36. Ibid., 265.

37. Wilder, *Theopoetic*, 56.

38. Ibid., 57.

darkness in the open earth, the vivifying of masks by theopoetics may lead to an inauspicious darkness over and against a pulchritudinous light, or it might merely be a vapid (or potentially pernicious) "getting high."[39] As such, one ought to remember that theopoetics is always a wager (Kearney)—or a perhaps (Caputo)—never a certainty. Wilder articulates it this way: "In a given situation there can be healing in intoxication as there can be *in vino veritas*. But madness is not always sacred. The powers of the soul can be dangerous. The daimonic may turn to the demonic."[40] Or we might say, the ecstatic trance can turn into escapism and the high to hierarchy. Once again Alves aptly conveys this promise and caution by noting the blurred line between drinking the Spirit and drinking spirits:

> But then, in a subtle moment, a reversal occurs. I no longer drink the wine. It is the wine which drinks me. I have been "drunk" by it. I am drunk. Now it is not the wine which enters my body. It is the wine which holds me inside a glass and drinks me, and I enter into a totally different world, a strange world which I don't know. My body is possessed by "spirits" which had remained outside till that moment. "In vino veritas": in wine truth abides . . . Pentecost: they were filled with the Spirit. They spoke and understood languages which had been unknown to them. And it was as if they were drunk.[41]

Thus, as one enters the arena of theopoetics the cautious player will remember that the masks vivified by poiesis, which enable new possibilities, new futures, and novel interpretations *to come*, may provide wonderful imaginative dreams that turn into reality, but the game might also provoke dreams that turn into nightmares! There are many ghosts afoot, left in beds and wandering highways! As such, the question will always linger as to whether the vivification is daimonic or demonic. Indeed, it will in a large part depend on what one is haunted by . . .

---

39. Alves, *The Poet, the Warrior, the Prophet*, 29.

40. Wilder, *Theopoetic*, 64.

41. Alves, *The Poet, the Warrior, the Prophet*, 14.

# Conclusion(s)?

*I remember, long time ago, I was fond of light. It happened, however, that by an accident, I became a friend to a poet. And I brought my texts to him to read. "—Too much light," he remarked, as if his eyes had been hurt by clarity. "Let's mix a bit of mist to your ideas, a bit of darkness to the argument, a bit of blurriness to the contours . . . Don't you know that a clear idea brings the conversation to a halt, whereas one unclear idea gives wings to worlds and the conversation never ends?"*

—RUBEM ALVES[1]

After exploring a nebula, being caught in a web, traveling at speed, surveying landscapes, flowing with a river, eating seasoned words, being guided by a flow, and delineating the pitch in order to continue playing the theopoetic game (an incredibly mixed metaphor—a bricolage indeed!), I find myself at the point of conclusion. Yet, my wish is that this is not a conclusion but possibly a beginning, or a coming again, or an eager waiting for the *to come*. My desire is that what is to come might not be a hopeless shot in the dark but rather a shot in the dawn. I yearn for that glimpse of first light to be an embodied and hopeful kick at the start of a new day, a poiesis.

I hope that you were convinced that we are situated in an intellectual time that is reeling from and grappling with rapid transit, movement, and flux—hauntingly explored by Kerouac—that dis-joints, dis-locates, dis-orders, and throws into question a number of long-held beliefs. Moreover, I hope you were persuaded that theopoetics is a discourse that is wrestling with the questions being asked by our culture—from

1. Alves, *The Poet, the Warrior, the Prophet*, 9.

practical imagination questions, to freeing liberation questions, to deep philosophical questions. Finally, I would be thrilled if by this point you are beginning to think that theopoetics, with its beauty, its play, and its daring movement into the future, is a relevant and viable way for engaging with and incorporating the divine into the questions of our time.

If you were at all persuaded, then I invite you to move into the future with theopoetics and me. It is my opinion that life requires a space in which to move and to be. If I am correct in my assessment, we need to welcome the future with openness to the possibilities that the flux might bring, but also we require a space in which to dwell if our ghosts and our bodies are ever to reunite.[2] I think that it is with an understanding of this dual need and a willingness to embrace both movement and dwelling that a grace-filled existence is possible. I see in theopoetics a discourse that fits the world's (specifically the postmodern West's) cultural moment, understands its questions, and adopts a posture of embrace rather than fear. I dream of assuming this stance because I want to move forward into the unknown in a posture of receiving the future as a gift (a grace, a contingent, a *Gelassenheit*), not with a disposition of fear that grasps for solidity. For me theopoetics' embrace provides a space from which to view and to experience one form of rationality's strongholds crumble and modern edifices melt into air. This space does not guarantee a good outcome, but it is a space in which new life might spring (both grow and flow) forth.

With an eye toward the spring, I share with a number of theopoets a reticence toward conclusions.[3] As Alves writes, "Conclusions are meant to shut (from the Latin 'con' plus 'claudere' to shut). . . . When thought appears stabbed to death one must be sure that the murderer was a conclusion . . ."[4] For, a conclusion cages up what ought to be left open. Resisting a requirement of putting words into cages, I follow Alves toward the body:

> Word and flesh,
> without separation,
> without confusion,
> and yet
> one single body.[5]

2. Kerouac, *On the Road*, 17.

3. Alves, *The Poet, the Warrior, the Prophet*, 9; Caputo, *Radical Hermeneutics*, 293–94; Keefe-Perry, *Way to Water*, 178; Keller, *Cloud of the Impossible*, 306.

4. Alves, *The Poet, the Warrior, the Prophet*, 9.

5. Ibid., 75.

Therefore, I would rather lose the conclusion and retain the incarnational tension. I nervously chuckle when I hear the satirical quip: *the Word became flesh, and we have done everything in our power to make it back into a word.* Instead I turn toward the body to resist this certain form of bibliolatry.

I also have refrained from offering conclusions in many of the above sections, and will refrain from tying a bow onto this gift of theopoetics. For more can be added to the gift and the gift will always exceed the bow one ties onto it. I tend to agree with Alves that to conclude would be to neuter, or render impotent, the *more* that might be said in each section. For as six *becomes* eight, as darkness *becomes* light, so too silence *becomes* speech. An end is always a returning to silence; after the end there is no more; only another beginning *to come*. As I release you, the reader, into this silent, incarnate, *becoming*, space, I trust Alves to be a better guide than myself. Alves in turn takes his lead from a rather well-known and well-liked theopoet: the Apostle John. It seems therefore most fitting that I should end by way of Alves's Johannine beginning:

> "The teaching about Christ begins with silence," says Bonheoffer
> in the first line of his Christology. And I imagine that a new
> prologue of the gospel of John could be written:
>
> "Before all things existed
> there was a great pregnant silence.
> And then, suddenly,
> 'ex nihilo,'
> a Word was heard,
> and the world began."
> "Ex nihilo" out of the Void . . .
> The Void is full of worlds,
> like the corpse of a dead man . . .
> The name of the dead man: was it Jesus Christ?
> The villagers, women and men, began to speak.
> Nothing about the dead man.
> Out of him.
> Because of his silence.
> Their speech was not an original act.
> They spoke because they heard.
> They heard words which were unknown to them:
> words which were not found in their stock of familiar knowledge.
> Their caged birds had no songs for the occasion.
> Wild birds, coming from forgotten regions—
> they did not even know that they existed!—

flapped their wings, feathers of bright colours,
singing songs unknown,
possessed their souls and bodies,
and they spoke—
like poets,
like magicians,
like lovers,
like theologians,
because theology is the Word which is spoken before the Void,
as an invocation of the Absent. . .
We dwell in forgetfulness.
The words we know are not our truth.
I think, therefore I am.
I am where I think.
But now the world is reversed.
Where I think, there I am not.
I am where I do not think.
I am where there is forgetfulness.
"We do not even know how to pray."[6]

6. Ibid., 33–34.

# Appendix

# Theopoiesis or Theopoetics?

| Author | Theopoiesis | Theopoetics |
|---|---|---|
| Stanley Hopper | X | |
| Amos Wilder | X | |
| Rubem Alves | X | |
| Gabriel Vahanian | | X |
| John Caputo | | X |
| Peter Rollins | | X |
| Catherine Keller | X | X |
| Richard Kearney | X | |
| Callid Keefe-Perry | X | |

***For the development and differentiation between these two terms please see pre-amble-ing where I discuss David Miller's "theopoetry" and "theopoetics" distinction, Catherine Keller's "theopoiesis" and "theopoetics" distinction, and the blurring of these somewhat false categorizations.

# Bibliography

Alves, Rubem A. "Eros, Language and Machismo: An Interview with Rubem Alves." *Cross Currents* 37 (1987) 456–60.

———. *The Poet, the Warrior, the Prophet: The Edward Cadbury Lectures, 1990.* London: SCM, 2002.

———. "The Protestant Principle and Its Denial." In *Faith Born in the Struggle for Life: A Re-reading of Protestant Faith in Latin America Today*, edited by Dow Kirkpatrick, 213–28. Grand Rapids: Eerdmans, 1988.

———. *Protestantism and Repression: A Brazilian Case Study.* Maryknoll: Orbis, 1985.

———. "Theopoetics: Longing and Liberation." In *Struggles for Solidarity: Liberation Theologies in Tension*, 159–71. Minneapolis: Fortress, 1992.

Barth, Karl. *Church Dogmatics.* Edited by Geoffrey W. Bromiley and Thomas F. Torrance. Peabody: Hendrickson, 2010.

Bockmuehl, Klaus. *Listening to the God Who Speaks: Reflections on God's Guidance from Scripture and the Lives of God's People.* Colorado Springs: Helmers & Howard, 1990.

Brueggemann, Walter. *The Prophetic Imagination.* 2nd ed. Minneapolis: Fortress, 2001.

Caputo, John D. *The Folly of God: A Theology of the Unconditional.* Salem, OR: Polebridge, 2015.

———. *Hoping against Hope: Confessions of a Postmodern Pilgrim.* Minneapolis: Fortress, 2015.

———. *The Insistence of God: A Theology of Perhaps.* Bloomington: Indiana University Press, 2013.

———. *The Prayers and Tears of Jacques Derrida: Religion without Religion.* Bloomington: Indiana University Press, 1997.

———. *Radical Hermeneutics: Repetition, Deconstruction, and the Hermeneutic Project.* Bloomington: Indiana University Press, 1987.

———. "Theopoetics as Radical Theology." In Faber and Fackenthal, *Theopoetic Folds*, 125–41.

———. *Truth: Philosophy in Transit.* New York: Penguin, 2013.

———. *The Weakness of God: A Theology of the Event.* Bloomington: Indiana University Press, 2006.

———. *What Would Jesus Deconstruct? The Good News of Postmodernism for the Church.* Grand Rapids: Baker Academic, 2007.

Caputo, John D., and Catherine Keller. "Theopoetic/Theopolitic." *Crosscurrents*, winter 2007. http://www.crosscurrents.org/Caputo0406.pdf.

Cobb, John B. *Whitehead Word Book: A Glossary with Alphabetical Index to Technical Terms in Process and Reality.* Claremont, CA: P & F, 2008.

De Gouvea Franco, Sergio. "The Concepts of Liberation and Religion in the Work of Rubem Alves." MA thesis, Regent College, Vancouver, 1987.

Derrida, Jacques. *Acts of Religion.* New York: Routledge, 2002.

———. *Of Grammatology.* Translated by Gayatri Chakravorty Spivak. Corrected ed. Baltimore: Johns Hopkins University Press, 1998.

Faber, Roland. "Becoming Intermezzo: Eco-Theopoetics after the Anthropic Principle." In Faber and Fackenthal, *Theopoetic Folds,* 212–35.

———. *God as Poet of the World: Exploring Process Theologies.* Louisville: Westminster John Knox, 2008.

Faber, Roland, and Jeremy Fackenthal, eds. *Theopoetic Folds: Philosophizing Multifariousness.* New York: Fordham University Press, 2013.

Feuerbach, Ludwig. *The Essence of Christianity.* Mineola, NY: Dover, 2008.

Fuller, Tripp. "The Birth of God and a New JC—Part 2 Keller AAR." Podcast from the American Acadamy of Religion 2014. http://homebrewedchristianity. com/2014/12/21/the-birth-of-god-and-a-new-jc-part-2-keller-aar.

———. *The Homebrewed Christianity Guide to Jesus: Lord, Liar, Lunatic . . . or Awesome?* Minneapolis: Fortress, 2015.

Gadamer, Hans-Georg. *Truth and Method.* Translated by Joel Weinsheimer and Donald G. Marshall. London: Bloomsbury Academic, 2013.

Guynn, Matt. "Theopoetics and Social Change." *Cross Currents* 60 (2010) 105–14, 137.

———. "Theopoetics: That the Dead May Become Gardeners Again." *Cross Currents* 56 (2006) 98–109, 141.

Halewood, Michael. "Reality, Eternality, and Colors: Rimaud, Whitehead, Stevens." In Faber and Fackenthal, *Theopoetic Folds,* 15–29.

Harrity, Dave. "The Theopoetics of Literature: An Aesthetic Statement, Part II." *Theopoetics* 1 (2015) 9–15.

Harrity, Dave, et al. "The Theopoetics of Literature: An Aesthetic Statement." *Theopoetics* 1 (2014) 5–10.

Hegel, Georg Wilhelm Friedrich. *The Philosophy of History.* Mineola, NY: Dover, 2004.

Heidegger, Martin. *Being and Time.* Translated by Joan Stambaugh. Albany: State University of New York Press, 2010.

———. *Discourse on Thinking: A Translation of Gelassenheit.* Translated by John M. Anderson and E. Hans Freund. New York: Harper & Row, 1966.

Higgins, Luke B. "Consider the Lilies and the Peacocks: A Theopoetics of Life between the Folds." In Faber and Fackenthal, *Theopoetic Folds,* 195–211.

Hocking, Jeffrey S. "Liberating Language: Rubem Alves, Theopoetics, and the Democratization of God-Talk." *Theopoetics* 1 (2014) 11–40.

Hopkins, Gerard Manley. *The Major Works.* Edited by Catherine Phillips. Oxford: Oxford University Press, 2009.

Hopper, Stanley Romaine. *The Way of Transfiguration: Religious Imagination as Theopoiesis.* Louisville: Westminster John Knox, 1992.

Huggins, J. Blake. "Introduction: Plato's Body." *Theopoetics* 1 (2015) 1–8.

Kearney, Richard. *The God Who May Be: A Hermeneutics of Religion.* Bloomington: Indiana University Press, 2001.

Keefe-Perry, L. Callid. "Theopoetics: Process and Perspective." *Christianity and Literature* 58 (2009) 579–601.

———. "Toward the Heraldic: A Theopoetic Response to Monorthodoxy." In Faber and Fackenthal, *Theopoetic Folds*, 142–58.

———. *Way to Water: A Theopoetics Primer*. Eugene, OR: Cascade, 2014.

Keller, Catherine. *Cloud of the Impossible: Negative Theology and Planetary Entanglement*. New York: Columbia University Press, 2014.

———. *Face of the Deep: A Theology of Becoming*. New York: Routledge, 2003.

———. *On the Mystery: Discerning Divinity in Process*. Minneapolis: Fortress, 2008.

———. "Theopoiesis and the Pluriverse: Notes on a Process." In Faber and Fackenthal, *Theopoetic Folds*, 179–94.

Kerouac, Jack. *On the Road*. New York: Penguin, 1976.

Laurent, Sam. "Kierkegaardian Theopoiesis: Selfhood, Anxiety, and the Multiplicity of Humans Spirits." In Faber and Fackenthal, *Theopoetic Folds*, 47–63.

Levinas, Emmanuel. *Totality and Infinity: An Essay on Exteriority*. Pittsburgh: Duquesne University Press, 1994.

Lieu, Judith. *Christian Identity in the Jewish and Graeco-Roman World*. New York: Oxford University Press, 2004.

Malbon, Elizabeth Struthers, and Edgar V McKnight. *The New Literary Criticism and the New Testament*. Sheffield: Sheffield Academic, 1994.

Marion, Jean-Luc. *In the Self's Place: The Approach of Saint Augustine*. Stanford: Stanford University Press, 2012.

Marx, Karl, and Friedrich Engels. *The Marx-Engels Reader*. Edited by Robert C. Tucker. 2nd ed. New York: Norton, 1978.

Mayers, Marvin K. "Protestantism and Repression: A Brazilian Case Study." *Journal of Psychology & Theology* 14 (1986) 249.

McGilchrist, Iain. *The Master and His Emissary: The Divided Brain and the Making of the Western World*. New Haven: Yale University Press, 2009.

Miller, David L. "Theopoetry or Theopoetics?" *Cross Currents* 60 (2010) 6–23.

Moltmann, Jürgen. *Theology of Hope: On the Ground and the Implication of a Christian Eschatology*. New York: Harper & Row, 1967.

Mounce, William D., and Robert H. Mounce, eds. *The Zondervan Greek and English Interlinear New Testament (NASB-NIV)*. Grand Rapids: Zondervan, 2008.

Myers, Ched. *Binding the Strong Man: A Political Reading of Mark's Story of Jesus*. Twentieth anniversary ed. Maryknoll: Orbis, 2008.

Nessan, Craig L. "Transparencies of Eternity." *Currents in Theology and Mission* 40 (2013) 59–60.

Nietzsche, Friedrich Wilhelm. *The Nietzsche Reader*. Edited by Keith Ansell-Pearson and Duncan Large. Malden, MA: Blackwell, 2006.

Pannenberg, Wolfhart. *Systematic Theology*. Translated by Geoffrey William Bromiley. 3 vols. Grand Rapids: Eerdmans, 1998.

———. "Theology and the Kingdom of God." *Una Sancta* 24 (1967) 3–19.

Phelps, Hollis. "(Theo)poetic Naming and the Advent of Truths: The Function of Poetics in the Philosophy of Alain Badiou." In Faber and Fackenthal, *Theopoetic Folds*, 30–46.

Provan, Iain W., et al. *A Biblical History of Israel*. Louisville: Westminster John Knox, 2003.

Reyes, Patrick Bruner. "Playing with Alves: In Memoriam: Rubem Alves (1933–2014)." *Theopoetics* 1 (2015) 87–93.

Ricoeur, Paul. *Interpretation Theory: Discourse and the Surplus of Meaning*. Fort Worth: Texas Christian University Press, 1976.

Rollins, Peter. *The Fidelity of Betrayal: Towards a Church Beyond Belief*. Brewster, MA: Paraclete, 2008.

———. *The Idolatry of God: Breaking Our Addiction to Certainty and Satisfaction*. New York: Howard, 2013.

———. *The Orthodox Heretic and Other Impossible Tales*. Brewster, MA: Paraclete, 2009.

Sobolev, Dennis. *The Split World of Gerard Manley Hopkins an Essay in Semiotic Phenomenology*. Washington, DC: Catholic University of America Press, 2011.

Sobrino, Jon. *Jesus the Liberator: A Historical-Theological Reading of Jesus of Nazareth*. Maryknoll: Orbis, 1993.

Stackhouse, John G. *Making the Best of It: Following Christ in the Real World*. New York: Oxford University Press, 2008.

Vahanian, Gabriel. *Theopoetics of the Word: A New Beginning of Word and World*. Edited by Mike Grimshaw. New York: Palgrave Macmillan, 2014.

Walton, John H. *Ancient Near Eastern Thought and the Old Testament: Introducing the Conceptual World of the Hebrew Bible*. Grand Rapids: Baker Academic, 2006.

Whitehead, Alfred North. *Process and Reality: An Essay in Cosmology*. Edited by David Ray Griffin and Donald W Sherburne. Corrected ed. New York: Free Press, 1978.

Wilder, Amos N. *Theopoetic: Theology and the Religious Imagination*. Lima, OH: Academic Renewal, 2001.

Wolterstorff, Nicholas. *Divine Discourse: Philosophical Reflections on the Claim That God Speaks*. New York: Cambridge University Press, 1995.

Zehnder, David J. "The Origins and Limitations of Pannenberg's Eschatology." *Journal of the Evangelical Theological Society* 53 (2010) 117–31.

Zimmermann, Jens. *Incarnational Humanism: A Philosophy of Culture for the Church in the World*. Downers Grove: IVP Academic, 2012.

Žižek, Slavoj, and John Milbank. *The Monstrosity of Christ: Paradox or Dialectic?* Edited by Creston Davis. Cambridge: MIT Press, 2009.

# Subject Index